About the Author

Toby Shelley is a journalist with the *Financial Ti*̴ ̴ast
twenty years he has reported from across A ̴
East. His previous books include *Nan*̴
and *Endgame in the Western Saharo* ̴e
Council of Management of th̴ ̴y War
on Want.

Exploited

Migrant Labour in the New Global Economy

TOBY SHELLEY

ZED BOOKS
London & New York

Exploited: Migrant Labour in the New Global Economy was first published in 2007 by Zed Books Ltd, 7 Cynthia Street, London N1 9JF, UK, and Room 400, 175 Fifth Avenue, New York, NY 10010, USA
www.zedbooks.co.uk

Designed and typeset in Monotype Jansen by illuminati, Grosmont
Cover designed by Andrew Corbett
Printed and bound in the EU by Gutenberg Press, Malta

Distributed in the USA exclusively by Palgrave Macmillan,
a division of St Martin's Press, LLC, 175 Fifth Avenue, New York, NY 10010

A catalogue record for this book is available from the British Library
Library of Congress Cataloging-in-Publication Data available

ISBN 978 1 84277 851 7 (Hb)
ISBN 978 1 84277 852 4 (Pb)

Contents

Acknowledgements

Thanks are due to the trade union organisers and the community workers who gave up their time and experience to talk to me. Their commitment is testimony to the determination of many in the labour movement and wider civil society to ensure that the rights of workers are respected, whatever their nationality or immigration status. Would that such principles were found in government.

Thanks are due to staff at Zed Books for their enthusiasm for my initial proposal and then for its successor. Family and friends have my gratitude for their support, encouragement and the occasional bright idea.

Introduction

Migrant workers surround us, doing jobs we shy away from, providing skills we no longer have, working hours we prefer to spend at home. The dainty pre-packed salad lunch from the supermarket was harvested by Portuguese workers and packaged by a Brazilian. A beer after work is served by a Slovak. The kitchen workers in the Chinese restaurant may have recently arrived from Guangdong province. The voices on the first buses in the morning are of Latin American and West African cleaners; the chatter on the building site is in Polish. The nurse is from the Philippines, the doctor from Ghana, the ward cleaner from Kosovo, and the security guard is a Kurd. Thousands of central Europeans have been recruited to drive those early-morning buses, while others keep the airports functioning, and the ships visiting our ports are crewed by seafarers of every nationality. Out in the harsh environment of the North Sea, Maltese and Cypriot workers are working on oil and gas projects while company managers wonder how to attract cut-price engineers from India or Russia.

France prides itself on its self-sufficient peasant agriculture, yet without Moroccan field workers many farmers would struggle.

In Spain it is African workers who can be seen cycling to distant orchards at daybreak and maintaining mountain farms. In the USA, great swathes of the construction industry and agriculture would grind to a halt without Mexican workers. Throughout the rich world, the better-off would soon be worse off were it not for the childcare services of domestic workers: au pairs from central Europe, live-in workers from Asia. In Oslo, the sex industry relies on transient international workers. Elsewhere, the economies of the Middle East gulf have been built and maintained on the backs of migrant workers from across Asia and poorer parts of the Arab world. In some countries in the region, migrant workers outnumber indigenous inhabitants. Egyptian and Palestinian engineers keep refineries operating. Building sites are worked by Pakistanis. In Bahrain the population is watched by a police force many members of which are Yemeni. In Thailand special economic zones have been established so the textile industry can benefit from cheap migrant labour from Burma, Cambodia and Laos.

Just as the migrant labour phenomenon that now attracts so much attention from politicians and the media is not geographically limited, nor is it new. French heavy industry has been propped up by foreign workers throughout the twentieth century. Southern Europe, which is now sucking in would-be workers from Africa and the Middle East, was long a source of labour to fuel the factories of the north, while the *Gastarbeiter* was as much a part of Germany as BMW.

However, political and economic developments have expanded the opportunities for labour and capital to 'meet in a global marketplace', to use the neutral language of economists. But for millions of potential migrant workers, what propels them to the marketplace is rather more compelling and traumatic than what persuades an employer to take on a batch of foreign workers. The collapse of the Soviet Union, the aggressive industrialisation and opening up of China, a string of wars in the Balkans and down the west coast of Africa were all seismic shocks that scattered multitudes into the 'global marketplace' to seek a more secure life, if not for themselves then for their families.

Technology has facilitated greater and greater, faster and faster integration of economies under a capitalist ethos, creating what one writer called 'The central confrontation of our time. That of the market against the state, the private sector against public services, of the individual against the collective, of egos against solidarities.'[1] Now deals can be discussed by mobile phone and formalised by email with funds transferred at the touch of a button. Goods and equipment are transported quickly and efficiently by container ships. Staff travel in airline seats while perishable goods – flowers from East Africa or exotic fruit from the Middle East – are stacked in crates in the hold. In such a world:

> Neither capital, nor work, nor primary commodities constitute in themselves determinant economic factors. What is important is the optimal relationship between the three. To establish this relationship, a company takes no account of either frontiers or regulations, only of the most profitable exploitation it can achieve from information, organisation of work and the revolution in management.[2]

Finance is truly international now. Foreign direct investment runs at around \$1 trillion a year, most of it accounted for by mergers and acquisitions between rich countries. Foreign investment in developing countries is highly concentrated, targeting Brazil, China, India, Mexico and the Russian Federation. The whole of Africa accounted for just 3 per cent of FDI in 2005 and again it is concentrated on a few countries, even a few deals. So, in that year, South Africa accounted for more than 20 per cent of the total due to a single acquisition by Barclays Bank. Most investment in the continent was by multinational companies expanding their grip on oil and metals resources as world prices soared.[3]

At the institutional level, the transition from the General Agreement on Tariffs and Trade (GATT) to the World Trade Organisation in 1995 heralded a more aggressive response to attempts by developing countries to shield sapling industries from the storm of global competition. All trade in goods, services, finance, intellectual property has come under the scrutiny of the WTO. Back in the late 1980s, while delegations limbered up for global trade negotiations, the Bretton Woods twins, the International Monetary Fund and the World Bank, were provoking the initial skirmishes of the 'central confrontation', imposing Structural Adjustment Programmes (SAPs) on the developing world, with resultant degradation of public services, destruction of economic sectors, and consequent unemployment and pressure to migrate.

So labour and capital meet in a marketplace where one party is in ebullient mood and the other traumatised. Capital can increasingly take its pick as to where it deploys. Hourly manufacturing wages in China are just a few per cent of those in the USA and under a third of those in Mexico, so even taking into account shipping costs it is easy to understand why operations are shifted from continent to continent.[4] The other side of the coin is that workers increasingly face the choice of working for non-negotiable wages and conditions on offer or travelling in order to find work that offers a sustainable life. The work that is on offer is, by and large, in those sectors where location is crucial, such as hospitality where a hotel is only useful if it is located somewhere people wish to stay, or construction where a building has to be put up where the client requires it, not where the labour is cheapest.

Of those who go abroad for work, some will settle permanently in the host country, becoming part of the wider community and facing long-term, often multi-generational challenges over equality of access to social provisions, cultural and linguistic identity – the sharp end of the debate over integration versus separation – though they may well not shake off many of the challenges faced by shorter-term stayers. Within this book, those who settle will be referred to as 'immigrants' and those whose stay is temporary as 'migrants'. But beware, some of the sources quoted do not make the distinction. And the definition is slippery because some arrive on a temporary basis and then decide to stay. Some arrive intending to stay and then decide against it. Others may never be conscious of having made a decision. There are Palestinian refugees from the 1948 expulsion who spent their lives waiting in vain to return to Haifa or Acre, seeing themselves as temporary residents in Britain. There are Polish workers who have been employed in Britain under the Worker Registration Scheme for a year and have already decided they want to relocate their families. Who is the immigrant and who the migrant?

A recent report on forced labour in the UK[5] set an upper time limit of five years in the host country as part of its definition of a migrant worker, whilst allowing a variety of forms of legal status. That time period seems to be a reasonable, if rough and ready, benchmark as naturalisation as a British citizen can only be applied for after five years of residence.

Of course, for some, primarily those privileged by education or with special skills, working abroad for a period brings wealth and other benefits. Migrants are some of the most highly paid employees in a country like Britain, but specialist lawyers and engineers, multilingual bankers and accountants, cutting-edge software developers are a tiny proportion of the total. The overwhelming majority are at the very bottom of the income ladder. That said, many workers in more mundane jobs consider it a fair exchange that they earn wages that are considered low in the host country but far exceed what they could expect at home. But if they are perceived to be undercutting local workers, there is another discontent to be considered.

This book does not concern itself with the fortunate few, the sought-after foreign employees who are encouraged to bring their families with them, even to convert from migrant to immigrant status by accepting a new crest on their passport. The subject of this book is not so much the use as the abuse of migrant labour. It argues that abuse is not only widespread but is part of the structure of key industries in the global North. It concentrates on the UK but the broad identity of sectors making widespread use of migrants across the North gives it a much wider relevance.

So what is the abuse? It is exploitation over and above the norm imposed on indigenous workers. Capitalism is driven by profit, and profit depends in large part on getting more out of a workforce than that workforce is paid. That is the exploitation of labour. It does not require a Marxist labour theory of value to recognise this. It is, as they say, a no-brainer. With the squeezing of the state sector even in health and education through subcontracting and public–private partnerships, less and less of society is protected from such exploitation. Clearly, the greater the productivity of workers – the higher the ratio of their output to their wages – the greater is the degree of exploitation. Migrant workers, like other vulnerable sections of the workforce, are susceptible to super-exploitation. They are more likely to accept low wages if those wages compare favourably with potential earnings at home. Their stint abroad is seen as a phase in their lives during which they may be prepared to accept some hardship to achieve an end. Often they are ignorant of their rights or are persuaded or tricked into waiving them.

It is important to see abuse of migrant labour as a continuum. At one end of the scale is the paring of conditions of employment, the stretching of working hours, denial of sick leave or holiday pay, allotment of jobs no one else wants to do, being switched from workplace to workplace, arduous travel. Towards the middle there are dramatic swings in working hours, fourteen hours a day one month and no work the next, gross underpayment, skimming of wages, excessive deductions for substandard accommodation and dangerous transport, fees for dubious services, isolation and workplace bullying. Further along yet, there is what amounts to bonded labour and other forms of forced labour where the worker is unable to walk away, perhaps because the employer or labour provider has indebted the worker or because of threats to hand him or her over to the immigration authorities, or the use of violence. At the furthest extreme are the children trafficked into rich countries to toil away their youth as domestic servants, and the women, children and men trafficked in for sexual exploitation and disposed of when no longer profitable.

Nobody would dispute that those last cases could be labelled modern-day slavery. Kevin Bales estimates there are 27 million slaves in the world today, generating some $13 billion a year. The overwhelming majority are found in the Indian subcontinent, with many more in Brazil and parts of Africa. But slavery, he argues, learns from and mimics trends in the broader global economy. It has shifted from ownership of labour to complete control. It has replaced slavery for life with seasonal slavery to minimise overheads.[6] And that slavery occurs in the towns and countryside in which we live.

Under international law what constitutes slavery is found further back along the continuum than the clear-cut victims of trafficking. The 1926 Slavery Convention defined slavery in terms of ownership, but in 1930 the International Labour Organisation Convention Concerning Forced or Compulsory Labour broadened the definition to include work not entered into voluntarily and extracted under threat. An ILO explanatory note says forced labour 'occurs where work or service is exacted by the state or individuals who have the will and power to threaten workers with severe deprivations, such as withholding food or land or wages, physical violence or sexual abuse, restricting peoples' movements or locking them up'. It gives as an example bonded labour, which occurs when the worker labours to pay off a debt to the employer but the value of the work is not fairly assessed, so the employer can extend the period of work at will. It also cites withholding of identity papers and threat of non-payment or violence if the worker is disobedient, and entrapment or kidnapping of workers by people traffickers.[7] These are only examples, albeit clear-cut ones. Often the menace may be more subtle – allowing workers to misunderstand their immigration status so they fear deportation if they walk out of a job; exploiting the social stigma at home attached to a woman forced into prostitution; indebtedness not to an employer directly but to an agency working with the employer; the tying of a job to accommodation. It will become clear that slavery in the global North is far more widespread than the occasional tabloid horror story of an imprisoned Asian domestic worker or a Lithuanian minor forced into prostitution.

For the labour movement there are clear interests in defending and extending the rights of migrant workers. On the level of principle, trade unions should not distinguish between workers on the basis of nationality and immigration status any more than colour or gender. For trade unionists and community workers, people have fundamental rights in the workplace, in the community and within any acceptable concept of justice that are not dependent on weighing a complex set of circumstances and motives that led them to a particular country. The categorisation of incomers as legal or illegal, regular or irregular, documented or undocumented, should not define rights. Abusive employment conditions are abusive whether they are imposed on a Slovak worker with an up-to-date work permit, a Jordanian student who has overstayed, or a Chinese worker smuggled into the country in the back of a lorry.

It may come as a surprise to some to learn this is not the view of the British Labour government whose minister for immigration in 2006, Tony McNulty, publicly denied that undocumented migrants have any workplace rights beyond the most fundamental human rights.[8] But looking at the wider context of UK government attitudes to migrant labour the sense of surprise fades. It will be argued that policy prioritises the policing of migrants over their rights and increasingly conflates issues of migration and immigration with law and order. At the same time it is adapting the migration regime in ways that will further racialise it and further erode workers' rights.

The architecture of the book is straightforward. It concentrates on Britain but makes extensive reference to other countries – migrant labour in domestic service in Italy and Spain, migrant prostitutes in Oslo, Mexicans in the USA, the rather different situation in Australian agriculture. The first chapter looks at the acceleration of migration and puts it into recent historical context. It touches on who migrates, why and how, and at what price.

The second chapter focuses on why and how migrant labour is used in industries and services where it is concentrated. It indicates the relationship between economic developments and the use of migrant labour in these sectors. It is also the part of the book that details the exploitation and abuse of migrant workers, ranging from those on North Sea oil platforms to women trafficked into the sex industry, food packers to contract cleaners.

Chapter 3 discusses the impact of migrant labour on the host economy and society. Migrant labour does bring benefits to the host economy, boosting national income and soaking up inflationary pressures. But that overarching truth may hide other less

Exploited

comfortable ones. The impact of migrant labour on the workforce in the host country is more complex and may be negative if employers are able to use migrants to price locals out of jobs or to worsen the conditions of those jobs.

Chapter 4 examines the strands of British government policy towards migrants – determination of who is to be allowed in, attempts to enforce that, and policing of conditions of employment. It finds policy and practice in all three strands to be woeful. Determination is on a path to allocation of job opportunity by race. Enforcement is cruel and doomed to be ineffective. The policing of employment is inept and gives low priority to workers' rights.

The Conclusion emphasises the importance of migrant worker issues to the labour movement and presents a provisional list of campaigning aims to transform government policy from obsession with migration as a law-and-order issue to enforcement of the rights of workers.

I

Migration in Context

Daybreak brought a massive new assault on the fence that
separates Melilla from Morocco. On this occasion, some 700
immigrants had taken part in the attack, demolishing the
fence, and some 300 had managed to enter Spanish territory,
according to the Civil Guard sources, despite the military
deployment that has supported the Civil Guard in manning the
frontier since last week. The incident took place at five in the
morning in the Chino neighbourhood zone, one of the points of
the Melilla fence that has been raised from three to six metres
… Four Civil Guards and three soldiers were variously injured
by rocks hurled by the attackers … Among the immigrants also
there were many wounded.[1]

It is the fourth assault in six days: a thousand immigrants tried
to get over the fence in two waves on the 27th of September;
650 at a single go tried it on Sunday … yesterday [the govern-
ment] announced the urgent construction of a new security
structure. This new fence will be placed around the exterior
iron fence and will consist of a series of metal bars embedded
in the ground and linked with cables.[2]

The imagery is clear. This is medieval siege warfare. Hordes of
the great unwashed hurl themselves at the ramparts of Europe,

using makeshift ladders to clamber over the defences of Spain's colonial enclaves in northern Morocco. Some 20,000 were waiting in Algeria, intending to make their way to Ceuta and Melilla with another 10,000 already in Morocco, according to the European Commission.[3] They use military tactics in their desperate efforts, say Spanish officials.[4] In the hinterland, in the hills and woods they mass their forces for the next assault, while Spain bolsters its defences and drafts in troops from the Spanish Legion. There are deaths. Five migrants died one morning attempting to get into Ceuta, at least three displaying bullet wounds that Spain blamed on Moroccan security forces.[5] They were not the only deaths in a drama that played out over weeks until the fences were too high and the numbers of defenders too great and the numbers of migrants depleted as they were repatriated by Morocco to Senegal, Guinea Conakry, Ghana and Mali, bundled over the Algerian frontier or abandoned in the Western Sahara.

Months later the militarisation of another border was under way to stem the infiltration of Mexicans and other Latin Americans into the USA. In a prime time television speech to the nation President George W. Bush said he would send 6,000 National Guard soldiers to the frontier, bringing the total to 18,000. The speaker of the house, Dennis Hastert, said: 'The decision to send troops is the shot in the arm we need to strengthen our borders and protect our families.'[6] By mid-September 2006, the House of Representatives had passed the Secure Fence Act, calling for 700 miles of fencing along the Mexico–US border. If Ceuta and Melilla recalled earlier depictions of European history, the militarisation of the southern extremities of the USA draws on the myths of the Old West, the Alamo, the right to bear arms cherished by unhinged survivalists and vigilantes alike. So, the Friends of the Border Patrol was formed in California to spot illegal aliens and ride horseback along the frontier. Already in Arizona there was the

Minutemen, an organisation that claims to be 1,000 strong, with accountants and publishers as well as ranchers in its membership.[7] It claimed its patrols, some of them armed, had cut illegal migration by 98 per cent in one month. It had plans to form groups in another nine states.[8] The increased militarisation of the frontier has pushed more and more would-be migrants to use the services of the 'coyotes' or people-smugglers, who have been able to raise their prices. Meanwhile, 500–1,000 people a year die trying to cross the border.[9]

August 2006: back to Spain's African outposts but this time the Canaries, lying offshore of the Western Sahara. Day in, day out, the front pages of Spanish newspapers are dominated by accounts of the arrival of overcrowded boats bearing sub-Saharan Africans on to the tourist beaches of the archipelago, 17,000 in eight months according to *El Periódico*.[10] Almost 1,000 people arrived in a single day in a flotilla of small, crammed *cayucos*, reported *El País*.[11] To the knowledge of the Spanish authorities, hundreds die attempting the crossing in a year, and no one knows how many bodies and overturned boats are never recovered. The journey has got longer as well. The route into the Canaries used to be through the Western Sahara, where criminal gangs benefited from the blind eye turned by Moroccan occupation forces. After pressure from Spain that route was sealed, so the operation switched as far south as Senegal. Madrid moved to block that route as well, but the boats will continue to depart from somewhere, Mauritania, Gambia or back to the Western Sahara, with bigger inducements for corrupt officials and higher prices for passengers. The journey takes about a week and only around half the vessels make it, the rest being turned back or disappearing into the Atlantic. A place for the perilous journey costs between $800 and $1,250.[12]

Another desperate sea route is undertaken from Tunisia and Libya to the Italian Mediterranean possession of Lampedusa, where over 10,000 would-be immigrants arrived between January and September 2006. Again, many never even arrive:

> Yesterday, the rescue teams recovered the bodies of 10 people and found alive another 70 who were travelling in a boat that overturned to the south of the island. The number of victims can be multiplied by four as 40 of the 120 immigrants who were travelling in the accident-hit sailing have disappeared.[13]

The drama of the storming of the fortifications at Ceuta and Melilla, and the pathos of the survivors of the boat crossings, well illustrate the lengths to which migrants from the global South will go to reach countries where they believe they can find work, opportunities for themselves and the means to support families at home. But they represent only a tiny fraction of the flow of migrant workers entering Spain without the required documentation. Catalonia was allocated 800 of those who arrived in the Canaries in the summer of 2006, just 0.3 per cent of the estimated total of immigrants without correct paperwork living in the region. By far the major route of entry is across the open border with France or through airports on tourist visas.[14]

In Britain the inflow of migrants has generally lacked the drama and the pathos of Melilla or Tenerife. That is not to say it lacks its horrors. The fifty-eight corpses found in a lorry in 2000 shocked the country, but who remembers, for example, the two who died of dehydration when they were dumped from a truck in rural southeast England in June 2006?[15] Migration has soared up the news agenda nonetheless. Until the closure of the Sangatte refugee camp in 2003, footage of refugees trying to board vehicles bound for the Channel Tunnel fuelled the panic over asylum seekers, many from Kosovo, entering Britain. But since the Blair government's crackdown on asylum seekers – boasting 'that removals of failed asylum seekers is at its highest rate ever, while asylum intake is at its lowest level since 1993'[16] – the spotlight has come to rest on those coming to Britain primarily to seek work.

Stereotypes, myths and obsessions

The considerable flow of workers from the European Union's 2004 accession states prompted media attention that produced a crop of headlines over the summer of 2006 from a chauvinistic press: 'Giving British jobs to foreigners is a recipe for national suicide' opined the *Daily Express*;[17] 'Jobless up 92,000 as Poles flood in', it had headlined the day before; and two days later it ran with 'Halt the tide of EU migrants … HIV children bringing timebomb to Britain'; the *Sun* managed 'Migrants get Brits' pay slashed by 50%';[18] while the broadsheet *Daily Telegraph* said 'Unchecked immigration is putting Britons out of work',[19] and reported the next week that since the Labour Party took power Britain had seen 'by far the highest level of inward migration in the country's history'.[20]

While the national press has largely concentrated on the impact of inward migration on the economy, not far below the surface lie other debates and neuroses. Former Labour minister Frank Field questioned whether current levels of immigration were acceptable. 'This is the most massive transformation of our population. Do we just merely accept this as another form of globalisation? That it doesn't matter where you are, or that you belong to a country and have roots? That we are all just following the jobs?' he said to the BBC news website.[21] Only the ineptitude of the far-right British National Party had prevented it from exploiting the situation, he added.

An obsession with a mythical national identity under constant threat from multitudes of incomers has been a feature of British political life since the end of the Second World War. Its expressions have ranged from the open racism of the 'No blacks, no Irish' notices in boarding-house windows and National Front 'martyr' Robert Relf, who advertised his house for sale to a white family only, through local opposition to the settlement of Vietnamese refugees in the 1970s, to the vilification of asylum seekers in the late 1990s. The inward migration of white central Europeans from the historically Christian accession states has not, by definition, fostered a racism based on skin colour or prejudice about 'alien' cultures, even if confrontation between migrants and members of the host community is reported in local newspapers. The received caricature of the Poles – by far the largest accession state community in Britain – is of hard drinkers and hard workers who fought with the British in the Second World War and suffered under Stalinism. But the stereotype built up of Bulgarians and Romanians as their countries' accession approached is more sinister – corruption, organised crime, HIV infection. This is something akin to stereotyping of Chinese migrants as either victims or members of snakehead gangs, Colombians as suspect drug smugglers, or Nigerians as fraudsters. It facilitated the decision to refuse Bulgarians and Romanians the same entry rights as citizens of Poland and the other 2004 accession states. Then there is the subtly encouraged demonising of the Muslim communities in Britain, which is an internalisation of the specious generalisations of the 'War on Terror'. Indeed, one suspects that with the waning grip of the 'War on Terror' and its attendant overseas adventurism and policy blunders on the popular imagination, the migration issue is being elevated to the status of next national crisis. The control of migration is a new governmental narrative, building on popular concerns, emphasising them, linking them to other anxieties like crime and security and then presenting 'solutions' to bind the electorate to the government. Margaret Thatcher, when she was prime minister, created the 'enemy within' from the trade union movement. The Blair government used 'Muslim extremists' and then undocumented migrants in a subplot. Linking the two are the demonised 'asylum seekers'.

It bears repeating that inward migration, far from imperilling Britain's identity (or set of identities), has actually defined it. What would Liverpool be without its close association with Ireland? And what of Bedford without the 10 per cent of the population that is first-, second- or third-generation Italian? A Birmingham without balti houses or hip-hop blasting from cars in Winson Green would be stranger to even a middle-aged white resident than being transported to Bucharest. To take another urban area, a study commissioned by the Learning and Skills Council focusing on the Thames Gateway (and also rural Norfolk) remarked,

> The very concept of 'migrant' poses difficulties in some parts of the Thames Gateway (especially in the East End). The whole area of the East End is traditionally a 'migrant community', and has been attracting migrants for many years: both past and present, it is a 'migrant community'.[22]

In media and political discourse there is a shifting hierarchy of incomers. Asylum seekers are divided between the ever smaller category deemed to be genuine political refugees the government has no option but to let through the door and the closet 'economic migrant' judged to be claiming persecution at best in order to find a job but most likely, according to tabloid innuendo, to feast on the bones of the UK welfare system. Other categories of economic migrant include those who have been smuggled into the country – either criminals or victims. Then there are the upfront migrant workers who come in from all over the world and are welcomed and valued until unemployment numbers rise or the number of incomers strains inadequate public services.

The distinction between political and economic migration is frequently specious. At the crudest level, how do you categorise someone seeking a better life than the increasingly grinding poverty induced by the persecutory political programme of the Mugabe regime in Zimbabwe? If an asylum seeker, once in Britain, seeks to work to provide for herself and remit money to family at home, does that render her an illicit economic migrant who should be deported or a potentially valuable member of society? A Chinese community activist asserts that there was a shift in the presentation of incomers from eastern Europe and China after the collapse of the Soviet Union. During the Cold War, the incomers were presented as defectors from repressive regimes. They were part of the ideological armoury of the contest. With the end of the Cold War and the establishment of strong economic ties with China, they no longer serve a political function and are characterised as economic migrants. This leads to the absurd situation where the long-term indigenous unemployed are condemned as scroungers but asylum seekers who seek out employment, personify the work ethic, are damned as frauds. Apparently, it is a test of political persecution at home that one submits to inactivity and impoverishment in exile.

Push and pull – why people migrate

There are push-and-pull forces at work in the decision to migrate. Jonathan Moses, in a book arguing for the abolition of border controls, points out that push factors must be powerful to drive people from their home:

> Most people, given the opportunity, will not choose to move from their family, friends and home. Indeed most immigrants yearn to return home and many eventually do. It is only under the most hopeless conditions that potential emigrants consider the exit option, and only a fraction of these have the character, contacts and resources to carry it off.[23]

Of course, the hopeless conditions to which Moses refers do exist in much of the world. Indeed the International Organisation for Migration calculates that 192 million people, 3 per cent of the world's population, live outside of their own country, a number that is growing at 2.9 per cent a year.[24]

People move from country to country for a variety, and often a combination, of reasons. Work is enormously important, but of official entrants into OECD countries in 2004, only in Switzerland, Denmark and Portugal did it account for over 40 per cent of approved entries. For Britain it was over 30 per cent. Families accompanying workers might be added to the category, boosting it somewhat. Family reunification is generally the largest category. Refugees account for less than 10 per cent of incomers to the OECD and the numbers have been driven down systematically since the early 1990s.

A paper by the UN's International Labour Organisation directly linked the rising secular trend in global migration for work to changes in the world economy: the disappearance of livelihoods through the loss of public-sector jobs, decline of traditional industries, loss of agricultural competitiveness, and the elimination of job protection because of World Bank Structural Adjustment Programmes. 'The evidence so far available on the impact of globalisation points to a likely worsening of migration pressures in many parts of the world.'[25]

For Liberians, Sierra Leoneans, Congolese, Angolans, just as for Kosovars and Chechens, Kurds or Colombians, in recent years the arguments for leaving home have been piled as high as the corpses. In parts of China, grinding rural poverty or the destruction of the artisanal fishing industry, plus the one-child policy, provide incentive enough for many breadwinners to take on huge debts with punitive penalties for non-repayment in order to travel to Europe or North America in the hope of bringing the family later. And the scale of the investment in sending a family member abroad is colossal. Sources interviewed for this book said people smugglers ask £20,000 to £30,000 for the trip from Fujian province in China to London, with 10–20 per cent paid upfront and often borrowed from a moneylender connected to the smugglers.[26] The payback period is typically between two and four years and the penalties for non-payment extreme. A Chinese Catholic priest who provided information for this book tells of burying a man in East London who had been beaten to death for non-payment. Members of a Turkish smuggling operation bringing people into Britain by boat, lorry or small aircraft were said at their trial to be charging £14,000 a head.[27] The going rate for taking a Mexican worker into the US was $2,000 to $3,000 in 2006.[28] The price of clandestine entry increases as the barricades are piled higher, so the sum just cited for a crossing into the USA includes a dramatic increase after the Bush crackdown,[29] while the price for being smuggled into France doubled after the Jospin government toughened up entry requirements.[30]

If the option under consideration is temporary residence abroad, the push factor need not be so powerful. (Indeed, for the young or unattached, it may scarcely exist – the adventure of seeking money and experiences abroad is enough.) A Chinese citizen migrating to work in Europe using one of the officially sanctioned employment agencies springing up in China might expect to earn £1,000 a month. That compares well with £100–300 a month in a factory in inland China, let alone the £100 a month a peasant in a prosperous region might expect. It even stacks up against the incomes in the coastal industrial belt.[31] Latin American migrant workers frequently come to Europe to save enough money to buy or build a house back home. Like their local counterparts, migrant prostitutes working in Oslo or London may well intend to amass enough savings to achieve a particular end – provide education for a child at home or pay off a family debt. Indeed, there is the apparent paradox that stricter border controls may well keep migrants in. In the USA it has been argued that the increased risks and costs of border crossing mean migrant workers are more likely to stay for longer or settle once they have arrived, whereas their parents and grandparents moved backwards and forwards relatively easily.[32]

For workers from the 2004 EU accession states, high unemployment and income levels that are low by EU standards provide push factors. Silesia used to be a byword for coal production but between 1998 and 2002, 100,000 miners were laid off. Of the 404,000 mine employees in 1989, there are now 123,000. An influx of supermarket chains has cut a swathe through the local retail industry. One young man was quoted as saying, 'Among my peers, half work abroad, mostly in London.' Another remarked of working in Ireland: 'By working on the high tension power lines I can earn enough to put some aside while living a normal life. With Polish salaries, in my profession, that would be unthinkable.' The region 'has 27 specialist colleges with a total of 150,000 students. An enormous potential that, unfortunately, is lost on the building sites of London and Dublin.'[33] With the average Polish wage only 20 per cent that of the UK, there is a clear financial incentive to spend a period working away, using the (relatively) easy entry that goes with EU membership and following in a line of Polish generations that have sought work abroad due to the political and economic conditions at home.

Even before the country's accession to the EU in 2007, migration was leaving parts of Romania denuded of young people, many of whom have gone to work in Spain. In the the village of Feldru 3,000 of a population of 8,000 have gone abroad, leaving it without people in their twenties and thirties.[34]

Even if the 2004 and 2007 accessions to the EU have smoothed the way for central European workers to find employment in the more prosperous member countries of the club, and global migration is accelerating, we should not forget that large-scale, organised labour migration within Europe has been taking place for decades. In the 1920s a French government body actively organised an inflow of workers for mining and heavy industry. In a decade 1 million workers arrived officially, with more arriving without the formalities. So, by 1931, foreign workers with restricted social rights accounted for 42 per cent of mine workers and 38 per cent of metal workers.[35] Between the 1950s and the 1970s, West Germany imported millions of temporary workers known as *Gastarbeiter*, without whom the post-war economic recovery would have been impossible. The largest group were Turks, whose government was paid a fee per worker, but Yugoslavs, Greeks and Italians were also used. We are reminded of this by Berger and Mohr's classic *A Seventh Man*, first published in 1975. The book details the process by which southern European peasants were transformed into factory fodder for the industrialised North.

More than three decades ago, Berger could write:

> In north-western Europe, excluding Britain, there are approximately 11 million migrant workers. The exact number is impossible to estimate because a probable two million are living and working without proper papers, illegally... The American business magazine, *Fortune*, states unequivocally that migrant workers 'now appear indispensable to Europe's economy'.[36]

In the same period the investigative reporter Gunter Walraff was writing about the use and exploitation of migrant labour in German industry:

> Five hundred workers – 80 per cent foreign – kept on their toes by Kurt Wokan and his 10 managers ... Wokan has a high opinion of foreign workers. He brings them in by the train load. Mostly from under-developed countries, mainly women, many of them illiterate.[37]

Of course, while there are factors that push people into seeking to work or live abroad, there must also be factors to draw them towards a particular destination. While family contacts or language or cultural affinity or misplaced notions of streets paved with gold may play their part, the primary factor is the well-grounded belief that the economies of the rich world have a hunger for the labour power of the developing world and the so-called transition economies. After all, demographic trends in the global North add daily to a labour shortage felt most acutely in labour supply for undesirable jobs. With an ageing workforce and declining rate of population growth, rich economies face a shortfall of local workers. As will be discussed later, without successive waves of migrant labour, frequently undocumented, the contract cleaning industry would be on its knees; without central and southern European agricultural labour supermarkets could not achieve 'just-in-time' stock policies; and without undocumented labour the Chinese and Indian catering industry would collapse. This is true across the EU. And in the USA undocumented migrant workers account for 24 per cent of farm workers, 17 per cent of cleaning workers, 14 per cent of construction workers and 12 per cent of those in food preparation.[38] As one US commentator summarised: 'It is important to recognise that, at this point in time, the US demand for im-migrant labour is structural in character. It is deeply embedded in our economy and society. The demand no longer fluctuates with the business cycle.'[39]

Globalisation and trade liberalisation, the ILO report cited above notes, have increased the demand as well as the supply of migrant labour:

> Small and medium size companies and labour-intensive economic sectors do not have the option of relocating operations abroad. Responses in these sectors include downgrading of manufacturing processes, deregulation and flexibilisation of employment, with

increased emphasis on cost-cutting measures and sub-contracting. In a considerable number of countries, these measures have expanded the number of jobs at the bottom of the employment scale. These jobs are referred to as the 3-D jobs: dirty, degrading and dangerous.[40]

With local workers frequently unwilling to take such work, there is a heightened demand for migrant labour. In North London the garment manufacturing industry thrived for a decade in the 1980s and 1990s on the labour of some 15,000 Turkish, Kurdish and Cypriot workers engaged in up to 1,500 sweatshops.[41] But the implementation of the deregulation deal at the Uruguay Round of world trade negotiations removed protective barriers and did so just as eastern European and then Chinese exports began to compete on the world market. The sector collapsed in Britain and now North London has perhaps fifty sweatshops, the capital from the rest having either been relocated to south-eastern Europe or transferred into catering and retail operations.

The immortal worker

In *A Seventh Man* Berger pointed to the clear advantages of employing migrant labour in the 1970s, and, as will be seen, for many workers from outside of the EU and, indeed, for some from within the EU, little has changed:

> The migrant worker comes to sell his labour power where there is a labour shortage. He is admitted to do a certain kind of job. He had no rights, claims, or reality outside his filling of that job. While he fills it, he is paid and accommodated. If he no longer does so, he is sent back to where he came from. It is not men who immigrate but machine-minders, sweepers, diggers, cement mixers, cleaners, drillers etc. This is the significance of temporary migration.[42]

He adds, 'So far as the economy of the metropolitan country is concerned, migrant workers are immortal: immortal because continually interchangeable.'[43] What Berger describes is commodification of labour taken to an extent that is no longer easy to achieve with the indigenous workforce, even after the mass unemployment and weakening of organised labour in the 1980s.

Migration for work requires resolve and initiative. Migrant workers are generally better educated, younger, stronger members of their home community who have decided to travel, albeit not in circumstances of their choosing. Jabez Lam, a community worker in London, rejects the victim–villain dichotomy in the official discourse about undocumented Chinese in Britain – 'trafficked' victim and villainous 'trafficker'. The reality is that the vast majority of undocumented Chinese workers in Britain and elsewhere in Europe and North America approach smuggling groups and enter into an agreement with them to pay to be transported. They are not coerced into migrating except by poverty. They are not trafficked, they are smuggled. And they do not travel in ignorance. The routes are well trodden, especially from Guangdong province. Others from their village will have gone before them and they will have a good idea of the risks they are running. Jabez Lam talks of a woman who had herself sterilised before migrating because she knew a friend had been raped en route.

He cites a case that he says demonstrates both the modus operandi of the smugglers and the determination of the migrants. It begins with a man agreeing to pay £20,000 to a group that will transport him to London. His wife and daughter remain in China and the agreement is that if he defaults the gang can claim either one of them. In London the man suffers severe depression and makes several suicide attempts, eventually being hospitalised long term. The gang go to his wife and say they will take the 3-year-old daughter for ten years in lieu of payment. She will be mutilated and set to work as a beggar. But they offer an alternative. The wife will be taken to London at the cut price rate of £10,000 and will pay off both debts. Once in London she finds three part-time jobs. In the early morning she washes up; then she works a split shift in a factory before cleaning in a hospital. She also provides some care for her mentally ill husband. The debt is repaid in four years, her husband discharged and they win exceptional leave to remain in the country and bring over the daughter. Asked about her experience, the woman said that she would do it all again, not least because by leaving China she had been able to have a second child. The point here is that for all of horror of the circumstances, this couple were active agents not passive victims in their own history, and they stand not only for the hundreds of their compatriots believed to arrive in London each week but for the majority of undocumented migrants.

In recent years, it has come to public attention that the health-care sector in Britain was systematically pillaging nurses and doctors from developing countries, particularly those with colonial links. Desperately needed staff trained in Ghana and South Africa were being tempted to Britain with the promise (often betrayed) of good jobs and salaries. (At the same time many central European medical professionals were packing warehouse shelves or picking fruit in the Midlands because their qualifications were not recognised, thus depriving their countries of the return on the investment made in training them and not even permitting them to practise in the country they travelled to.)

This too is a structural part of the migrant labour phenomenon. Berger, talking about the 1970s again:

> It has been estimated that the upbringing, the price of survival to the age of 20 of a migrant, has cost the national economy of his own country about £2,000. With each migrant who arrives,

an underdeveloped economy is subsidising a developed one to that amount. Yet the saving for the industrialised country is even greater. Given its higher standard of living, the cost of 'producing' an 18 year old worker at home is between £8,000 and £16,000.[44]

If globalisation has generated new demand for and supply of migrant labour, then, in an age of trade liberalisation and deregulation, why is it that global labour mobility has not been negotiated? There are bilateral deals between neighbours, frequently formalising reality rather than creating new conditions, and there are multilateral agreements between members of trading blocs but labour movement liberalisation does not figure in the priorities of the World Trade Organisation. Movement of goods and services is negotiated. Arguments lumber on over the mutual reduction of subsidies and tariffs protecting agriculture or steel production. Multinational companies are able to assert patent rights over seed varieties developed over generations by Indian farmers. All in the name of free trade and its trumpeted but often elusive advantages.

By definition it is the laws that limit entry to a country that make criminals of those who try to enter. It is then the status of illegal entrant that enables undocumented workers to be exploited because they have little recourse to action. Further, the smuggling networks that bring in undocumented migrants, often for extortionate prices in dangerous conditions, only exist because there is no legal route. As a report already cited remarks:

> employers and migrants are willing to pay increasingly higher prices to meet each other in an internationalised labour market. Increased migration control and restrictions contribute to making circumventing restrictions a lucrative field of activity to respond to market pressures, making trafficking and smuggling of migrant labour very profitable.[45]

So, by inhibiting free movement of labour, governments create two classes of criminal – the worker and the smuggler. While the worker is unlikely to present any threat to society – he or she simply wants a job – people smuggling may involve or accompany a range of other activities, including smuggling of contraband goods and unlicensed gangmastering.

A fundamental criticism of British government policy is that it reduces the economic and political reasons that force many people to seek work abroad to a narrow, domestic law-and-order issue. Having done that, it becomes 'acceptable' for a government minister of a party that once claimed socialist and internationalist leanings to assert that undocumented workers have no workplace rights. This plays well with the xenophobia of the right-wing press and its constituency, and complements or even demands related policies such as 'cracking down' on asylum seekers.

However, just as politicians maintain distinctions between the 'deserving poor' and the 'undeserving poor', the 'unfortunate' and the 'indolent', so the need to offer something to the socially liberal wing of the electorate forces them to recognise a small proportion of undocumented entrants as 'victims' deserving of sympathy, even if the help they then receive is paltry or non-existent. Foreign women 'rescued' from prostitution are deemed to be victims of trafficking (even if they are then deported as illegal immigrants), but there has been no recognition of the smuggling of children as domestic labour. Chinese migrants may be portrayed as victims of organised crime although they have not been trafficked, may have a nuanced relationship with those who smuggled them in, and much of the hardship they may endure in Britain results directly from government policy.

In the part of his book arguing for free and unfettered international migration, Jonathon Moses presents rational economic reasons why host countries should open their borders – economic growth, greater public finance, positive impact on the general standard of living.[46] All these make perfect sense. Amid the days and weeks of front-page coverage of the migrant boats landing on the Canaries came the report that Spain's economic growth rate over the past decade grew by 2.6 per cent a year due to migrant labour, without which it would have fallen by 0.6 per cent a year.[47]

Certainly there are political considerations involved in limiting inward migration, such as the repercussions of perceptions – true or false – that migrants take jobs from natives and lower wage levels, or fears that migrant labour will transmogrify into large immigrant communities with different cultural and linguistic traditions. But there is also good reason to believe that the very migration that governments of the rich world make illegal they also tolerate, in effect colluding with exploitative employers.

What Moses argues may be correct long-term in the macro-economic environment but the interests of political policymakers and businessmen are much more likely to be served by shorter-term considerations. What will emerge, time and again, is that the use of undocumented labour is systemic in various sectors of the economy. In some instances this is because of local competition; in others it is because of international competition. Generally, it is tied to the immobility of the business, an immobility due to lack of resources needed to relocate, or to the nature of the business – a cleaning company has to be where the buildings that need cleaning are. Where international competition is responsible for the use of undocumented labour (or, more generally, the forcing down of wage rates), the liberalisation of the movement of goods and services that seemed logically to demand liberalisation of movement of labour can be seen to have exactly the opposite impact. Trade liberalisation, compounded by structural adjustment policies, has created a bigger pool of people desperate to improve their circumstances through migration, while simultaneously the pressures of competing with lower-cost rivals abroad may have made employers in some sectors more likely to take on cheaper, undocumented labour. Removing undocumented status would raise wages and so be inimical to employers.

For all the rhetoric, without massive expenditure it is not even conceivable that the increase in the number of undocumented workers could be halted, although the flow could be regulated to some extent. We have already encountered the argument that in the USA tighter border controls keep undocumented labour in the country. And throughout the global North, with numerous businesses from high street restaurants to contract cleaners to food processors and security companies dependent on undocumented workers, collusion is a far easier path for civil servants and politicians to tread. Writing about migrant labour in France, Morice Alain sees 'the integration of the clandestine immigrant into the economy as a necessity, but also a transformation of the economy so it functions in anticipation of clandestinity'.[48]

The UN's International Labour Organisation puts this argument even more strongly:

> numerous governments informally tolerate irregular migration while they officially reinforce controls against 'illegal' migrant workers. The effects are, on the one hand, a continued supply of cheap labour, while on the other hand, 'illegal' migrants are unable to organise in the workplace to defend their dignity and decent work conditions, stigmatised and isolated as well from allies and support.
>
> The practices of many states of tolerating the presence of migrant workers in irregular status to meet labour needs in certain sectors of the market constitutes a de facto employment policy in which part of the workforce becomes a variable which can be reduced or even eliminated (in theory) in periods of economic downturn, through exercise by states of their prerogative to expel foreigners from their territory.[49]

Migratory tides

Estimating net flows of population in and out of even rich, techno-logically endowed countries whose borders are relatively easy to monitor or difficult to cross is an imprecise art. Natives leaving must be netted off against incomers and returnees. The arrival of short-term visitors must be matched against their departure. Those who intended to stay might not and many who arrive as tourists or students will overstay. Then there are those whose category changes while they are in a country. And, on top of that, there are those for whom no records exist. Some of them may have destroyed their identification documents on arrival at an airport and others will have entered a country illicitly, stowed away in a lorry, on a boat, clinging to the underside of a train.

Numbers of undocumented entrants vary widely from country to country but for some countries are believed to be as high as 3 per cent of the total population. In Italy and Portugal, for example, large numbers of undocumented immigrants render the official sta-tistics meaningless. In the USA it is estimated that undocumented entrants into the country since 1990 totalled well over 11 million by 2005, with 40 per cent arriving in the 2000–05 period, at a rate of 850,000 a year.[50] Of the total, some 7.2 million were believed to be employed, amounting to 4.9 per cent of the civilian workforce.[51] As far as the official numbers for documented net flows into Britain go, the trend is rising, from 60,000 in 1999 to 250,000 – 66 per cent of the total population increase – in 2004–05 and most of that accounted for by accession-state nationals of working age, 'a significant boost to the UK labour supply'.[52]

Bureaucracy complicates matters for all concerned. These com-plications can leave a migrant believing his or her status is legal when it is not or, as trade-union organisers and other note, that it is not when it is. There are more than fifty different official bureaucratic procedures by which someone can come to Britain to work or study. The most important for our purposes are outlined later.

Definitions of migrant and immigrant vary not only from country to country but also between agencies in the same country. If the numbers themselves are suspect, the trends are clear none-theless. An important source of comparative data is the annual International Migration Outlook published by the OECD using official national data and looking at movement in and out of the richer countries of the world. As its 2006 edition noted:

> immigration flows grew rapidly in the 1990s and are now growing again … There are currently close to three million long-term immigrants entering OECD countries legally every year, and even more temporary movements … And this does not count unauthorised movements.[53]

Non-native-born workers are a growing proportion of the OECD workforce, albeit with big variations between countries, as little as 1.5 per cent in Japan and a staggering 25 per cent in Switzerland with Germany coming in at 12 per cent.[54]

Leaving aside long-term entrants – immigrants as I choose to define them – with whom this book is not so concerned, there has been a widespread growth in the numbers of workers entering OECD countries under temporary schemes. The increase was 7 per cent from 2003 to 2004, reaching 1.5 million, just for those countries with detailed figures and excluding students who are permitted to work while they study.[55]

Australia is a case apart because there governments have con-centrated on attracting immigrants rather than migrants, and where temporary migrant labour has been imported the emphasis has been on specific skills. Nonetheless, the number of work visas issued rose to 700,000 in 2004–05 from under 100,000 a decade earlier.[56] The unskilled element comprised not migrant workers from the Pacific islands or Indonesia but rather young people on working holiday visas, backpackers and the like. Even this raised the ire of sections of the labour movement and proposals to allow Chinese workers into the country to work in agriculture and the meat-processing industry met fierce opposition.[57]

Migration flows change over time, according to political and economic developments, although geographical proximity and historic (often colonial) links often form core currents. Berger omitted Britain from his study in the 1970s on the grounds that the inward flow was dominated by the legacy of empire rather than the erosion of a south European peasant agriculture.

A London builder, himself a fragment of the long-standing flow of Irish labour into Britain that went into reverse in the 1990s, remarked that he did not need to read a newspaper to know which parts of the world were suffering turmoil; all he had to do was listen to the languages spoken by men in search of casual work. Again, in the London construction industry, where in years gone by an unexpected need for extra labour was met by a trip to Cricklewood to recruit a van-load of Irish workers, in 2006 the van would turn up at one of a handful of streets in West London to collect a batch of Polish workers.

The collapse of the Soviet Union and associated governments from 1989 brought new trends in migration into western Europe. The OECD report notes a rise in asylum seeking, fraudulent entry and overstaying soon after. Germany then took in ethnic Germans from central Europe and, since accession to the EU, hundreds of thousands of Poles, Slovaks, Lithuanians and others have moved to Britain, Norway and Ireland and elsewhere. The multiple conflicts in the former Yugoslavia created overlapping waves of emigration while other countries of southern Europe, such as Italy, long net exporters of people, became destinations for migrants from the Middle East and Africa. Increased emigration from Latin America, sometimes sparked by internal conflict such as that in Colombia, has made Spain a first port of call for large numbers because of colonial and resultant linguistic ties, even if many then fan out into other EU countries, sometimes ending up as undocumented cleaning workers in the City of London. Others head north for the USA where 22 per cent of undocumented entrants are from Central America.[58]

The inflow of foreign population to the EU, Norway and Switzerland has risen steadily since 1999, from some 1.6 million then to 2.8 million in 2004.[59] For the UK the rise was from 287,000 to 494,000, a little under the average in percentage terms. By far the largest inflow to Britain was from Australia, with France, Germany, India, South Africa and the USA all figuring high, demonstrating the predominance of proximity and historical links in determining migration paths. Far from the UK being overwhelmed by non-English-speaking, dark-skinned asylum seekers, the bulk of in-comers were Europeans or of European origin, many with English as a first or second language and many with UK antecedents. The exception was China, which has soared up international rankings of inflows in recent years as travel restrictions have eased.[60]

Concomitantly, the population of people holding different nationalities from that of their host country has risen in percentage terms across much of the OECD. These figures exclude people who have been naturalised and, obviously, those who have entered illicitly. But the increase for many countries is not dramatic. In Sweden the proportion fell in the decade to 2004. In Germany, long a major importer of *Gastarbeiter*, the fluctuations have been minor. For Ireland, the economic boom of the 1990s meant the proportion of foreign nationals in the population doubled to 5.5 per cent in the period. Italy, Portugal and Spain saw greater rises. For Britain the proportion grew from 3.4 per cent in 1995 to 4.9 per cent in 2004, from some 1.9 million to 2.9 million, the largest contributing nationality by far (albeit in decline) being Ireland, followed by India, the USA and Italy. The last year for which the OECD report provides data is pivotal in terms of inflow to western Europe, being the year of accession of Poland and the Baltic states to the EU.[61]

It will now be useful to look briefly at the channels through which documented migrant workers enter the country that this book focuses on, the UK, because the conditions attached to each determine the workers' rights in the country. There are four main official methods of entry at the time of writing.[62] Business and commercial work permits for senior managers, employees with scarce skills, and intra-company transfers are not dealt with because these privileged migrants – whose numbers grew 10 per cent to 137,000 in 2005 – are not the subject of this book.[63]

In principle, EU nationals have free access to the labour market. In fact, most older EU member states used terms of the accession to exclude from their labour markets accession-state workers. Britain, Ireland and Sweden did not do so, although Britain passed legislation to control access. The Worker Registration Scheme was brought in to allay fears that hordes of central Europeans would flock to Britain to claim benefits rather than work. Under the scheme, a worker pays £70 to register and must provide a letter demonstrating he or she has work arranged. The worker pays national insurance and tax and has full employment rights. After twelve months of continuous employment, the worker is entitled to the same rights as, say, a Portuguese worker (seasonal Portuguese labour has long been important to parts of British agriculture). Those claiming to be self-employed do not have to register.

The number of people registering under the Worker Registration Scheme, as opposed to the government's woefully poor prior estimates, formed the basis of much of the furore over migrant labour in Britain in 2006. In the two years to June 2006, 427,000 applications under the scheme were approved. Taking into account the self-employed, the government rounded up the number of accession state workers believed to be in the country to 600,000.[64]

The Seasonal Agricultural Workers' Scheme for those outside of the European Economic Area allows students to work on British farms for up to six months at a time. They may be switched from employer to employer during that period. They are supposed to receive the minimum wage and pay no more than £27 a week for accommodation. By 2005 the numbers on this scheme had fallen to 16,250 from 25,000 a year before as accession-state students switched to the Worker Registration Scheme. The scheme was originally introduced after the Second World War to ensure a flow of young labour into agriculture during the post-conflict disruption.

The Sector Based Scheme was phased out at the end of 2006. By then it only applied to parts of the food manufacturing industry. It was withdrawn from the hospitality sector after evidence of abuse. The purpose of the scheme was to provide labour for low-skilled, hard-to-fill vacancies. Workers from outside the European Economic Area were eligible and could stay for twelve months at a time with the possibility of extensions.

In January 2002, the Highly Skilled Migrant Programme was launched as a pilot. It is a points-based system and the migrant applies rather than an employer. The permit lasts for twelve months. After four years, the holder can apply for permanent residence. On top of this, the almost 300,000 students coming to Britain each year are entitled to work part-time. Asylum seekers may work if their claim is still outstanding after twelve months. The extension of the period from six months has probably driven many into unsought illegality.

By definition, figures for those present outside of the rules are best-guess at most. A paper on irregular migration by the

Institute for Public Policy Research recently cited government estimates that ranged from 310,000 to 570,000, based on 2001 census statistics.[65] Not all of this number may be in the workforce in either the formal or the informal economy, but at the same time the range is probably too low because the census numbers are now old and, furthermore, incomplete.

Working from Labour Force Survey Data, a study for the Office for National Statistics looked at the stock of foreign workers in Britain and calculated that it rose above 1 million in 1998, reaching some 1.5 million in 2005, 5.4 per cent of the total workforce. Of these, 45 per cent were European, with 31.7 per cent coming from EU or European Free Trade Association states.[66] As sections of the press rushed to say, this number was an all-time record. What the report emphasised was that there was no immediate way of telling how long incoming workers would stay.

Notionally, the equation for calculating the stock of migrant workers would read something like: the sum of those entering the UK under the four outlined schemes plus those not required to register under the Worker Registration Scheme because they are self-employed, minus those leaving. Add to this overseas students engaged in part-time work, minus those returning home, plus a proportion of asylum seekers working legally. Then add the universe of irregular workers (a catch-all that includes everything from overstaying tourists to victims of trafficking and smuggled workers with no documents), minus those detained or deported.

The rapid influx of accession-state workers has radically changed the profile of the population of foreign nationals in Britain and altered the profile of the migrant labour community even more. If the government's 600,000 figure is correct, then the number of accession-state nationals actually *working* in Britain in 2006 exceeds the number of Irish nationals *living* here in 2004. Indeed the number of registered Polish workers, at 265,000 in mid-2006, would make them the biggest foreign community apart from the Irish, and the number excludes those who have declared themselves freelance, let alone dependants and students.[67] The proportion of the workforce with Irish nationality almost halved between 1995 and 2005.

To put the phenomenon of accession-state influx in perspective, in the late 1990s a noted feature of migration into Britain was the increasing flow of (generally well heeled) Australians and South Africans. For 2001, the total number of people admitted to live in Britain from those two countries was 46,600.[68]

It is an open question whether accession-state workers will remain a transient, migrant community or evolve into an immigrant community, grafted on to the Polish and Czech communities that have lived in Britain since the middle of the twentieth century. Estimates of those intending to stay for two years or more vary from 4 per cent to 40 per cent. The government points to the proportion of registered workers who have their dependants living with them, which rose from 6 per cent in the middle of 2004 to 12 per cent two years later.[69] A survey carried out for BBC's Newsnight programme found one in seven Polish workers saying they intended to settle permanently in Britain and one-third saying they had family with them.[70] At a trade-union office in Lincolnshire, where many Poles are employed in agriculture, officials said as many as one-third might wish to remain in Britain long term. That as many as 5,000 births were registered by the Polish consulates in Britain in a single year has also been held out as evidence of families settling.[71]

Geographic distribution of migrant workers has been skewed towards London and the south-east of England, accounting for 47 per cent and 20 per cent of the total, respectively.[72] However, recent data suggests a marked change in distribution trends, at least among accession-state workers. In the second quarter of 2004, some

25 per cent of Worker Registration Scheme applications were for London; after two years the proportion had fallen to 9 per cent and the highest number of applications was for the Anglia region, which now has the highest number of workers registered under the scheme, some 65,000 or 15 per cent. London comes second at 14 per cent and the Midlands at 12 per cent.[73]

So, migration is on the rise across the globe as those disadvantaged by poverty and conflict seek a better life for themselves and their families. As the consequences of climate change, largely generated by the global North, become apparent the trend will continue upwards as competition for resources sharpens. The quest for work is a major, primary impetus and, even for those whose first thought is simply to escape the battlefield, the need and desire to achieve a reasonable standard of living through employment is likely to follow quickly on. This is all the more the case because the difficulties and costs of migration are such that it is the young, the determined, the educated, those with initiative and courage who take the risks. Although to different degrees, this is true for those taking a bus from Silesia bound for Dublin and for those smuggled from one end of the earth to the other.

That migration for work is on the increase should not disguise the fact that it has long been a factor in the economies of the global North, whether the factories and mines of France or the orchards of California. Who moves and where they move to are factors strongly influenced by changes in the global economy to which the migrant falls victim – the collapse of small-scale agriculture in southern Europe, unemployment caused by structural adjustment in Africa, the collapse of the coal industry in much of Europe.

But migrants are not simply propelled from their own country. They are sucked into their countries of destination, and not because they are foolish or ignorant enough to believe the streets

Exploited

are paved with gold but because of the demand of particular industries at particular times, be it the shortage of labour in French agriculture in the late 1940s, the West German industrial boom of the 1960s or the need for labourers on Irish mushroom farms today. Employers seek cheap, willing labour and migrants fit the bill. It is no surprise that the loudest voices defending the influx of migrant labour into the UK have come from employers' organisations.

Yet, already disadvantaged as supplicants for permission to enter and to work, migrants are further disadvantaged and their bargaining power weakened by a complex of distinctions and divisions. Pre-2004 EU-member citizens have one set of rights, 2004 accession-state citizens another set, 2007 accession-state citizens another. Yet different conditions attach to Commonwealth members. Migrant labour is sliced and diced into the legal and illegal, the documented and undocumented, those with desirable skills and those without. Rigidities in the system demand that someone comes either for economic reasons or for political reasons, with the former sifted through the laws and regulations and the latter actively discouraged from working to support themselves. But while those who work without official sanction, be they asylum seekers or smuggled workers, are actively criminalised, their status simply makes it more profitable for unscrupulous employers to use them.

Migrant Labour

Across the world there is a broad overlap in the sectors in which migrant labour is used. The harvesting of agricultural produce and major construction projects, by their very nature, have always required swing capacity, and the seasonal nature of fruit picking or hod carrying, or catering for the tourist season, has militated towards informality in workplace arrangements. That informality opens the way to avoidance of norms and regulations, and to the introduction of extreme forms of exploitation, be it through dangerous working practices or low pay. In some industries the scale and volatility of demand for labour have been exacerbated by heightened competition, either local or more distant.

Demand for migrant labour can be divided into two broad categories: that for raw labour and that for more specific categories of worker, perhaps with particular skills or, in some sectors, of a particular race. There can be an overlap between the two categories, created or perpetuated by local conditions; so, although cleaning work on the London Underground requires undifferentiated, unskilled labour, in fact it is dominated by particular nationalities, probably due to word-of-mouth recruitment. Within the cruise-ship and hotel businesses there is often a division of labour by race and gender.

A number of industries are examined in this chapter. In some, like the food industry, migrant labour is almost entirely used for unskilled or semi-skilled work. In others it is more mixed. There are disproportionate numbers of Polish labourers on UK building sites, but there are also bricklayers and, indeed, very specialised workers from abroad. The sectors dealt with here are the ones where migrant labour is geographically widespread among the rich countries – agriculture, hospitality, cleaning, domestic work, construction, seafaring. That does not mean that local conditions do not have a major role in determining the specifics – they do. In construction, for example, the tax regimes in the UK and Italy are relevant. In the case of the North Sea oil industry the demand for migrant labour has come about through a particular combination of macroeconomic factors that prompted short-sighted changes to recruitment and training practices.

The sex industry is a bridge between various other categories of economic activity. Laws vary widely from country to country, but broadly speaking the sex industry spans the legal and the illegal, the formal and the informal economy, the documented and the undocumented worker. It can also merge with parts of the domestic labour business. And one of the facets that makes public discussion so fraught, and brings the sex work–prostitution debate of academics down to earth, is the spectrum of conditions across which workers in the industry operate. This ranges from content, cosmopolitan free agents through to the grossly abused, trafficked and enslaved. Not to differentiate between the two would be as irrational as not distinguishing between a migrant working as a security guard for a reputable company on regulated wages and conditions, and the case of the young man (detailed below) taken on, exploited and cheated by a disreputable security company.

We are accustomed to thinking of the sex industry as inhabiting a grey area that straddles the legal and the illegal. But we should not forget that many vulnerable workers, among them migrant workers, in a range of industries, inhabit that grey area. Workers, particularly if they are undocumented, may work in food-packing plants where the produce is sold for cash to restaurants and market stalls without tax ever being paid. They may work under the fiction of self-employment on a building site, or as nannies for middle-class parents who do not pay their national insurance contributions, or sell pirated DVDs on city streets.

The following sections narrow the focus from the overall stresses and strains in the global economy that create the phenomenon of migrant labour to look at the structures of particular industries, how and why they generate demand for migrant workers and the conditions they impose on them. This is where poverty in rural China, unemployment in Poland, orphanhood in Nigeria are transformed into the use and abuse of people we sit next to on the bus in the morning or rub shoulders with in corner shop.

The Food Industry

The seasonal nature of agriculture, with high labour demand during harvest time in particular, has always necessitated the use of temporary labour. Changes in the supply chain of the food industry have exacerbated this. In many countries, the increasing use of migrants rather than locals to do this work is linked with the flight of rural-born people from agriculture.

In Greece, where some 17 per cent of migrant workers are engaged in agriculture, a study concluded that

> migrant labour has contributed positively in the past decade to
> the avoidance of an impending economic and social crisis in

agriculture and country life by filling labour deficits and reducing labour costs. Migrants have also offered farm families opportunities to reallocate family labour.[1]

Research into the employment of African migrants in Spanish agriculture associated the phenomenon with the switch in some areas to more labour-intensive crops and to the 'negative tones and low social status' of agriculture as urban values spread to the countryside.[2] The ILO found that in Italy the use of seasonal migrant labour had become 'a fundamental component of Mediterranean agriculture', replacing marginal Italian workers in temporary labour as well as working in greenhouses and on livestock farms.[3]

In the USA, where seasonal agricultural labour markets are very varied, 'Foreign-born newcomers play a particularly significant and growing role in the hired crop workforce', with the proportion rising from 10 per cent to 16 per cent of the total in the decade to 2002.[4] On the other side of the Pacific, farmers in parts of Australia use a combination of retirees, backpackers, students and undocumented migrants from Asian and Pacific countries to fill labour gaps made worse by the reticence of the children of farmers and farm workers to enter the industry. There have been calls to allow asylum seekers to work in agriculture and for the importing of workers from East Timor, Papua New Guinea and China.[5]

A generation ago it was common for school-age children to be employed alongside women without regular jobs to pick potatoes in England. Student labour was and is taken on in the guise of 'working holidays' for the raspberry season in Scotland, and East Anglian orchards have taken on all comers to pick apples. With the mass unemployment of the 1980s, cash-in-hand farm labour was attractive to many former industrial workers. But by the mid-1990s falling unemployment rates and a crackdown on benefit fraud had driven many native-born temporary agricultural workers away from the industry just at the time when demand for a compliant, cheap and disposable workforce was building.

This has been easy work for migrants and immigrants to secure, with little in the way of language or training requirements. Pay rates are low, often with stated or implicit deductions for accommodation, but piece work enables the young and fit to increase their income. From the 1960s onwards, agricultural and allied food-packing work was important to the Sikh, Pakistani, Kashmiri and Yemeni communities settling in Birmingham and the Black Country. They would travel out to Worcestershire and the Vale of Evesham with their work arranged through gangmasters. Since the influx of 2004 accession-state workers, the immigrant community workforce has been squeezed out by the new migrant wave. According to Zad Padda, now a consultant to the food industry but previously manager of a packing house and a gangmaster, employers cite a 'better work ethic' on the part of the new arrivals, but he suspects they prove easier to control, less aware of their rights and cheaper. Indeed, he says workers from the urban Asian communities are now having to accept less than the minimum wage in order to secure work.

Perhaps because agricultural and food industry work is a staging post for those seeking longer-term employment or intending to settle, this phenomenon of one nationality replacing another has been seen elsewhere. North Africans are slowly being replaced by Bulgarians and Romanians in Spain, while Ukrainians, Romanians, Moldovans and Russians are edging out lusophone Africans in Portugal.[6] Meanwhile, Portuguese labour has been used on farms and in packing houses from the English West Country to the East Midlands and East Anglia at least since Portugal joined the EU in 1986. While that source remains important, it too has been pressured by the influx of workers from the 2004 accession states. There are some 30,000 to 40,000 migrant workers in

Lincolnshire, mostly engaged in agriculture and in food packing and processing. Until 2004 they were almost entirely Portuguese with an admixture of many other nationalities, including Brazilian, Kurdish and Iranian. Indeed, market towns like Boston have proportionately large settled Portuguese communities now. Since 2004, however, the balance has shifted and perhaps half of the migrant community is now Polish.

A profile of the migrant community in the Breckland area of Norfolk describes 'a clear polarisation between a more established migrant worker community (in our case Portuguese), which is characterised by older migrants with lower levels of education and generic skills, and a more recent community which is increasingly of eastern European origin, young, middle class, well educated and skilled.'[7] Indeed, in Breckland while 79 per cent of migrants were employed in low-skilled jobs, 75 per cent of them had occupied medium- to high-level jobs at home and 15 per cent had been in management or professional posts.

Statistics from the Worker Registration Scheme should, in theory, show the relative importance of different industries to migrant workers. In fact, the catch-all category of 'administration, business and management', accounting for 34 per cent of worker registrations between the second quarter of 2004 and the second quarter of 2006, obscures the reality because it is a generic term used to cover workers employed by agencies for a variety of occupations.[8] Nonetheless, agricultural workers, even excluding those hidden by the catch-all category, accounted for 12 per cent of registrations, over 50,000 workers with food and fish processing accounting for another 5 per cent or 21,400 workers.[9] The short-term nature of the employment is clear. While 49 per cent of all registered workers were in temporary jobs, for agriculture the proportion was 69 per cent.[10] This makes the sector particularly likely to seek and to attract migrant workers, and this is borne out by a focused study on the employment of temporary workers in the sector. The number of temporary workers on farm enterprises in a given month was assessed at 224,713.[11] However, the temporary nature of the work and the turnover of staff mean that the actual pool of labour was estimated at between 420,000 and 611,000 workers,[12] so far more workers pass through the sector in, say, one year than are seen in a snapshot of a given day. Surveys in 2004, on the cusp of accession by the central European states, showed that 43.7 per cent of the temporary workers in the sector were UK nationals, with 23.5 per cent from other EU countries and 32.5 per cent non-EU.[13] With the accession, the proportion accounted for by EU states will have risen sharply and the non-EU category shrunk accordingly.

The difficulties of organising agricultural labour are notorious in the trade-union movement. In the nineteenth century they were recorded by the likes of Joseph Arch and Joseph Ashby. Enormous problems exist today: the temporary nature of much of the work; the geographical isolation of workplaces and workers; the tendency for accommodation to be tied to the job; the lack of alternative work in rural areas. For migrant workers these problems are frequently compounded by unfamiliarity with the language and the law. It is no surprise that it is from the agriculture sector that the most constant flow of tales of abuse and exploitation of migrant workers originates.

The abiding problems in securing workers' rights are compounded by changes in the structure of the food chain brought about by the overbearing influence of the big supermarket corporations and their buyers. When Tesco alone accounts for over 30 per cent of Britain's annual household spend on foodstuff, its power in the market is immense. But Tesco and its rivals are in a constant battle for market share. In part that battle is fought through acquisitions, so Wm Morrison bought Safeway for £3.35

billion in 2004, and Wal-Mart, the notorious US-based corporation (the world's largest retailer), bought Asda in 1999 for $10.8 billion. Another weapon in the armoury is aggressive price competition, particularly the introduction of the Everyday Low Price strategy that aims to keep the cost to the customer of a basket of goods lower than competitors' all year round rather than using temporary promotions on particular items. For example:

> In 2001 Asda slashed prices by £52 million and announced the first of 400 'Smart Price' food products based on Wal-Mart's new £450m budget brand. In the first five years since being bought by Wal-Mart, Asda's grocery market share has increased from 13% to over 16% without acquiring any new stores.[14]

Thus, it is not the shareholders who pay for the price cuts: it is suppliers, who in turn try to reduce their costs, and migrant workers, who pay in the end.

There has been a similar consolidation of corporate power among the food service companies that supply caterers. Just as the corner shop and the independent high-street retailer have been pushed to the brink by supermarkets, so the local firms that supplied restaurants and canteens have seen their business undercut by global players like Compass and Sodexho. And companies like those continue to drive down their costs, and that means wages. As Compass said in its annual results presentation for 2006: 'We will work closely with clients and employees to improve labour scheduling and efficiency, contain wage and ancillary cost inflation and to reduce unit overheads.'[15]

In order to compete with each other the supermarkets and the food service companies drive down their own costs. A variety of methods are used to achieve this. Just-in-time ordering, based on more and more sophisticated forecasting of demand, reduces warehousing costs and shifts the burden of ensuring the right goods are in the right place at the right time to logistics companies that are themselves in cut-throat competition to win and keep contracts.

The number of buyers employed by supermarkets has fallen, according to the Precision report,[16] sometimes by increasing outsourcing. This results in a concentration of financial power, a greater distance between the buyer and the producer, and so, arguably, an ability to plead ignorance about the situation on the ground. For the food producer, the overwhelming dominance of the big supermarkets and service companies all seeking to squeeze down costs means that contracts must be safeguarded no matter what. To have higher costs than the farm or packing house next door is to put commercial survival in jeopardy because the all-powerful buyer is under instructions to pare costs further. And farmers' costs have been increasing, driven by the rise in energy prices of recent years. (Even the niche market for organic produce, for which a premium could be charged, is now coming under the same pressures as the supermarkets deem the niche to be big enough to warrant serious attention.) British farmers in 2004 received 25 per cent less for their contribution to a basket of food products than they did in 1988.[17]

Trade liberalisation plus the development of a global transport infrastructure that can import flowers by airplane from sub-Saharan Africa or prepared chicken from Southeast Asia on refrigerated ships means that producers are competing not only with their neighbours but with farms thousands of miles away. Home-produced fruit and vegetables now account for well under 40 per cent of the total consumed in Britain.[18] On top of that, commentators have suggested that pressure for serious reform of EU protectionism in agriculture has incited further fears about global competition.[19] It is not only European farmers who feel the chill wind of global trade liberalisation. Mares notes Australian growers' concerns about the strength of their dollar when they are competing against producers with lower labour costs in Chile and South Africa.[20]

The reaction of farmers, food packers and processors, and indeed the supermarkets themselves, to the intensification of competition between the retail giants has been to reorganise labour in a drive to make it more flexible in the face of stop–start demand, and cheaper. This has led to a massive increase in the use of part-time labour in the sector in Britain, up from 25 per cent of the total in the early 1980s to some 50 per cent now.[21] It has also created the circumstances in which the use of migrant labour flourishes. Some 90 per cent of agency workers in secondary food processing are migrants,[22] according to a study for the agriculture ministry. And, just as the chance to pay cash-in-hand to the unemployed of the 1980s was seized upon by many food producers keen to trim the wage bill, so the competitive pressures faced now mean many employers and labour providers will find ways of paying below the minimum wage if they can do so, sometimes through the use of undocumented labour and sometimes by creating the sort of competition for work that Asian agricultural and food-sector workers in the West Midlands face.

The same process can be seen in continental Europe. Alain writes:

> France is the most developed country in the world when it comes to supermarkets and equally it is France that is the primary source of orders for fruit and vegetables from Spain. People order at two in the morning at the market and the vegetables must arrive in the evening or early the next day. We see the results: Say I am a grower. Today I will need 20 Moroccan workers to harvest my strawberries, tomorrow I might need 50 and the day after that 100 but the next day none.... This is what happens in Europe, not just Andalusia.[23]

Since 1999, booming mushroom-growing horticulture in Ireland has taken on several thousand women workers from eastern Europe and Asia via agencies. Some of them are being paid one-third of the legal minimum, piece rates have been squeezed down, and they face large deductions for accommodation. Additionally, they face the peril of exposure to dangerous chemicals.[24]

The gangmaster

The gangmaster has been a familiar figure in English agriculture for many years. Historically, the role began in the east of England in the sparsely populated fenlands only relatively recently drained for agriculture and where settlements were previously islands poking above the waters of the fens. In the first volume of *Capital*, Marx powerfully describes the gangmaster's role as found in East Anglia and the East Midlands in the mid-nineteenth century:

> The gang consists of 10 to 40 or 50 persons, women, young persons of both sexes, ... and children of both sexes.... At the head is the gangmaster, always an ordinary agricultural labourer, generally what is called a bad lot, a scapegrace, unsteady, drunken but with a dash of enterprise and *savoir faire*. He is the recruiting sergeant for the gang, which works under him, not under the farmer. He generally arranges with the latter for piece work, and his income, which on average is not very much above that of an ordinary agricultural labourer, depends almost entirely upon the dexterity with which he manages to extract within the shortest time the greatest possible amount of labour from his gang...
>
> The gang system ... clearly does not exist for the sake of the gangmaster. It exists for the enrichment of the large farmers, and indirectly of the landlords. For the farmer there is no more ingenious method of keeping his labourers well below the normal level, and yet always having an extra hand ready for extra work, of extracting the greatest possible amount of labour with the least possible amount of money, and of making adult male labour 'redundant'.[25]

Gangmasters are still dominant in these areas of England. Estimates gathered for this book, from the Citizens' Advice Bureau in the region, of the proportion of migrants employed through gangmasters ranged from 70 per cent to 98 per cent.[26] But over time, their geographical reach has spread. In the Vale of Evesham in the west of England there were estimated to be 1,000–1,500 workers employed through gangmasters in 2004.[27] Indeed, the advantage it offers to farmers and packer – labour to order – means similar systems have been seen cropping up in recent years in continental Europe, the USA and Australia.

The connotations of the term 'gangmaster' mean that few labour providers describe themselves as such, preferring to call themselves 'local employment agencies'. At the same time, many generic employment agencies have moved into the provision of labour for agriculture and food packing. The British legislature defined a gangmaster as someone who supplies or employs workers directly or through another person to a labour user in the agricultural, shellfish-gathering or food-processing industries. Inasmuch as they do this, 'employment agencies' or 'employment businesses' as defined in the 1973 Employment Agencies Act may be gangmasters and require licensing as such.[28] This definition, along with the legislation it framed, has been much criticised, as will be seen in Chapter 4. It also flies in the face of common parlance where a gangmaster is a local, small-scale operator, probably only active in this business for a part of the year and very possibly informally.

Labour providers are intrinsic to the structure of agriculture and farm-based food packing. The farmer has always required a surge of labour at certain times of the year, principally around harvest, but has not wanted the costs of retaining that labour. Changes in the food supply chain have added new volatilities to the demand for labour, to the benefit of those who can supply it. So, the House of Commons committee on the environment, food and rural affairs concluded that the dominant position of the supermarkets in relation to their suppliers is a significant contributory factor in creating an environment where illegal activity by gangmasters can take root. Intense price competition and short time scale between orders from the supermarkets and deliveries to them put great pressure on suppliers who have little incentive to check the legality of the labour which helps them meet these orders.[29]

The Citizens' Advice Bureau made similar observations, saying of the increasing use of documented and undocumented labour in the food industry:

Sometimes such employment is direct but more often than not it is through sub-contracts with one or more employment agencies or, in the agriculture, food processing and cleaning sectors especially, gangmasters. Many of these agencies and gangmasters are all too ready to engage in poor and illegal employment practices – indeed some are clearly run as criminal enterprises. The activities of such unscrupulous middle men can soon lead to a downward spiral of wages, conditions and workplace safety with even good employers facing irresistible pressure to cut corners and ask no questions in order to make a profit.[30]

The manager of the West Norfolk bureau commented: 'The gangmasters/agencies seem to employ those workers with least in the way of immigration and benefit rights as they are more likely to be intimidated.'[31] The Precision report calculated that of the almost 225,000 temporary workers on farm enterprises at any one time, more than half – over 125,000 – were recruited by labour providers.[32]

Estimates for the number of gangmasters operating in Britain have ranged up to 3,000, but others argue that 1,000 is nearer the mark. In its first year of operation, the Gangmasters Licensing Authority received almost 1,000 applications and issued over 640 licenses. A locally commissioned report suggested that the changes in the farming and food industry were squeezing out the smaller player and benefiting larger-scale labour providers. Zad Padda, whose family supplied Asian workers from the West Midlands to farmers and packers in the surrounding countryside, argued that traditional labour suppliers such as his father were being pushed out by the arrival of high-street-name employment agencies importing workers from central Europe.

While the gangmaster or agency acts as provider of local labour to relatively local employers, the scope for profit is limited to a cut of the fee agreed for the work. But where migrant labour is involved there is much more room for enrichment and this is where much of the abuse of migrant workers takes place. Where the local worker is self-sufficient, the migrant is in need of a range of services, from accommodation to transport to banking, and labour providers have ensured they exploit this need.

Exploitative labour providers are not a feature solely of the British food industry. In southern Italy the daily labour market per-sists, according to the ILO, which noted that labour 'bosses', often non-Italian nationals themselves, took on workers, took them to an employer and hired them out at a higher rate. The workers are paid piece rates below the rates paid to irregular Italian labourers.[33] In the Dordogne region of France, North African migrant workers pay €5,000–10,000 for their job, the sum being divided between the employer and a recruiter, a practice that amounts to bonded labour.[34] In Australia there are signs that gangmastering in the British style may be developing,[35] and in California it seemed to re-emerge as a means of combating advances made by organised labour.[36]

At the Grantham community branch of the GMB in the heart of Lincolnshire farming country, union officials described the use of tied accommodation and transport to skim wages and to tie migrant workers to labour providers. At the same time, workers are frequently employed without legal contracts. Nine out of ten workers who ask an employment agency to see a contract are fired on the spot, according to Cheryl Pidgeon, East Midlands regional organiser.

A common practice has been to import workers and then keep them without work for several weeks. Meanwhile, they are housed in accommodation supplied by the labour provider, building up a debt of £500–600 on top of any debts they have incurred for transport to Britain. This amounts to bonded labour. The worker cannot leave because of accrued debts he or she neither wanted nor can pay off. The labour provider controls the worker in a manner that fits the international legal definition of slavery and that certainly accords with Bales's notion of modern forms of slavery – short-term, adapted to the demands of a modern economy. Then, sums of around £150–300 are often paid for transportation and assistance in finding work. The GMB cites instances of the transportation being across Europe in the back of an unroadworthy truck and the assistance comprising being dumped in a Lincolnshire field or shown the door of a Job Centre.

Once a debt has been incurred, the worker is tied to the labour provider. On the minimum wage, with deductions for accommodation, and trying to remit money back home – the motive for those with families migrating in the first place – such debts are very difficult to pay off. Once debts are almost paid off another period of enforced unemployment can see them build again, while control over the worker is sometimes exerted illegally by holding his or her passport as security, a practice that constitutes forced labour in the eyes of the ILO.

For some labour providers it is very likely that the profits made from accommodation actually outstrip those made from supplying workers. A Polish GMB organiser in Grantham interviewed for this book said that a house can be rented commercially in the town for £500 a month. Cram in ten people at £50 each per week and that gives a profit of over £1,500 a month per property. Some local gangmasters control several houses, and workers have been charged as much as £90 a week. In extreme cases so many migrant workers on shifts have been using an address that they have had to 'hot bed', with the same bed being used by different people throughout a 24-hour period. This environment is conducive to intimidation. The GMB office reports the case of a Portuguese woman housed with seven men who sexually harassed her.

The demand for housing to accommodate migrant workers is so great that in late 2006 it was cited as a reason for the boom in buy-to-let property prices in Wales. 'With payments of £65 to £80 per week per room being the norm, this is proving very attractive to investors', an estate agent told the *Western Mail*.[37] Accommodation provided by employers as opposed to labour providers has also stirred controversy. Tesco and Sainsbury have both said they would look into union allegations that S&A Produce, a major strawberry supplier, was cramming up to ten workers into caravans while working them long hours on low pay. The company denied the allegations. The previous year 300 workers had blocked a road to complain about pay and conditions.[38]

The short-term nature of the work brokered by gangmasters and others means that the place of work often changes and this can entail long journeys, sometimes two or three hours a day each way. Ashbourne in Derbyshire takes workers billeted many miles away in Birmingham or Stoke-on-Trent. It has been common practice for migrant workers to be charged for this transport, sometimes as much as £5 a day, a substantial amount for people earning the minimum wage. It is not unusual for the drivers to be line workers already tired after a day's work or a poor night's sleep in overcrowded housing. Little wonder there are accidents. Six people, five of them migrant workers, were killed in a crash in mid-February 2006 in Lincolnshire,[39] the third fatal accident involving migrant workers in the county in six months. In July 2003 three Kurdish workers were killed when their van collided with a train on a level crossing in Worcestershire, where they had been employed by gangmasters to pick spring onions.[40]

Like other migrant workers, those in the agriculture and food sectors are also prey to a variety of other illegal deductions such as fees for being registered with the Home Office, management fees and charges for setting up bank accounts or applying for national insurance numbers.

The GMB officials in Grantham said the £5.20 an hour minimum wage that workers should have been receiving often ended up as £3 an hour after deductions. After sending home what they can to their families, some workers wound up living on £10 a week. The Citizens' Advice Bureau in Boston, Lincolnshire, said in November 2003 it had a client who was left with just £6 a week after deductions.[41]

Morecambe Bay

The deaths by drowning of 23 Chinese cockle pickers in Morecambe Bay, Lancashire in February 2004 laid bare the depth of exploitation of the lowest grade of migrant workers in the agriculture and food industry, the undocumented and failed asylum seekers. Prior to the deaths, the authorities' interest in what was happening on the beaches of Morecambe Bay, Swansea Bay, the Burry Inlet, Dee Estuary, the Thames, the Wash, and Solway Firth was limited to the occasional raid by immigration officials and police.

Two years later, three Chinese held responsible for the deaths and for being gangmasters to the victims were jailed, while the English businessmen who purchased cockles from the pickers were cleared of breaching immigration law by employing illegal migrants. That it was Chinese people who were convicted allowed perpetuation of the notion that responsibility for the deaths lay with people smugglers, the snakehead gangs of the popular imagination. Indeed, after the trial, the policeman who led the investigation fuelled the misunderstanding by portraying the whole sorry tale as one of immigration crime rather than exploitation of labour: 'I hope lessons have been learned but it's not about just cockle pickers, it's the whole issue of illegal immigration. It's a truly awful type of slave trade, exploiting people in this way.'[42]

In her essay looking behind the deaths, Hsiao-Hung Pai puts the cockle-picking tragedy into its true context, one of gross exploitation of migrant labour. The workers took up the work due to a variety of situations typical of irregular migrant workers. For one his work in a takeaway did not pay enough for him to remit money home. Others had been laid off due to the seasonal nature of the work they had been doing before. Others lived in fear of immigration raids at previous workplaces – all 23 were failed asylum seekers, asylum seekers awaiting decisions, or unknown to the authorities.

Gangmasters found the Chinese workers to be productive, punctual and cheap.

> Chinese cockling was initiated and developed into a profitable
> business … by a layer of prosperous local cockling middlemen
> who supplied seafood processing conglomerates. They controlled
> the workload required and set production targets for the 30–40
> Chinese cocklers in each team, and were referred to as 'bosses',
> supplying companies such as Penclawdd Seafoods Ltd (owned
> by Dani Foods). Contrary to public assumption, the incoming
> Chinese cocklers recruited since 2002 were making huge profits
> not for their smugglers but for Dani Foods.[43]

Payment was delayed by the labour users. Health and safety was never a concern to labour providers or users, and tide timetables were not issued. So it was that a gang was sent out at night against the tide to gather two lorryloads of cockles, to be transported to Spain where the Galician industry had been ruined by an oil-tanker leak.

Hsiao-Hung Pai quotes the Chinese man who would be convicted of manslaughter railing against the system in which he became a minor player: 'The ultimate responsibility for the Morecambe Bay deaths lies with the top bosses, the English suppliers and their international clients who put enormous pressure on us to produce.' Another of those convicted asked, 'Tell me – if the big bosses didn't demand a harsh production target, why would any Chinese workers give up their time off and work like hell cockling on the Yuan Xiao night [a Chinese festival], the night they died?'

In the wake of the tragedy local employers across all sectors became nervous that officialdom might take a greater interest in irregular Chinese workers, and a number were fired summarily, according to a community activist. But the cockling continues, now with Polish gangs...

Exploited

The Citizens' Advice Bureau is often the first or only recourse for migrant workers in rural areas, and they have extensive case-based knowledge of the problems faced by their clients. The GMB officials interviewed estimate that one in five migrant workers in their area face very severe exploitation. This is a shocking figure, suggesting that tens of thousands of workers are suffering extreme poor pay and conditions. And the union officials' views were supported by the results of a survey of bureaux in rural areas of eastern England carried out for this book. They indicated the widespread presence of conditions conducive to forced labour, modern-day slavery. Of the four bureaux that provided extensive answers (Boston, West Norfolk, Fenland, and South Holland), all said that on more than ten occasions in the previous twelve months they had encountered cases where migrant workers had been paying excessive deductions. They also each said they had encountered more than ten instances of non-payment of due wages. The same was the case for workers accruing debts to gangmasters or employers that they were unable to repay. This is prima facie evidence of gross exploitation shading into forced labour on a substantial scale. Each of the bureaux also reported more than ten known instances of verbal intimidation of workers by employers, gangmasters or other workers in the period, and more than ten instances of physical intimidation. In this atmosphere, union officials do not attempt to visit farms and packing houses but rather contact workers out of hours through Internet cafés, bars and churches. GMB officials have been threatened by gangmasters and employment agency proprietors.

Needless to say, the work done by migrant workers in the agriculture and food sector is repetitive, generally unskilled, and often physically demanding. Hours are uncertain. Frequently, if they have the benefit of a contract, workers will be obliged to opt out of the Working Time Directive so longer hours can be squeezed out of them. But just as likely are periods of under-employment, with consequent loss of earnings and accumulation of debts. An organiser for the Transport and General Workers' Union in South Wales said that the main problem he faces is the use of 'zero hours contracts' by a major local employment agency that brings in Polish labour for food-processing work that local workers refuse because of the pay and conditions. In the contracts signed by migrants, the agency says it will endeavour to provide 48 hours of work per week but does not guarantee it. New arrivals are worked for 12, 14 or more hours a day on the minimum wage rate with no overtime bonus. After a few months they are moved on to a later shift, but can be told when they arrive that there is no work for them because it is being done by more recent arrivals on the earlier shift. Sometimes this has gone on for weeks at a time. Meanwhile the workers are building up debts of £50 a week for rental charges and £25 a week for transport, let alone living expenses. They become short-term bonded labourers unable to change agency or employer-cum-landlord until the latter decides to allow them enough work to pay off accrued debts.

Control of migrant agricultural and food-processing workers through manipulation of their immigration status has been report-ed by trade unions, in the press, and in individuals' testimonies. One Citizens' Advice Bureau reported that the practice was very common in 2004 but had become less so since then (perhaps due to the regularisation of the status of an estimated 100,000 workers from the 2004 EU accession states). In some cases, terms and conditions will simply be worse than for workers with the correct paperwork. As in other sectors, there are accounts of selective raids on workplaces just prior to payday with the detention of one group of workers while another group is left unmolested although equally irregular in status. Indeed, while there is no more than circumstantial evidence, some people working to support irregular migrants argue there is complicity between some gangmasters and some immigration officials.

The *T&G Record* interviewed someone working in a detention centre who said:

> We are beginning to get the feeling there is some sort of protec-tion going on... A rumour may go round that a farm is about to be raided. That day the illegal workers disappear, probably on the advice of their gangmaster. The raid is carried out, the workers escape, the target for raids is met and the gangmaster keeps his workforce... But some gangmasters 'grass' their own workforce. They want them deported because they have wrung most of their

money out of them, and it seems as if Immigration has been happy to oblige, plucking some workers but not others from the production line.[44]

Again, it should be stressed that while Britain is the case study used in this book, the same methods of exploitation, entrapment and sometimes enforcement of labour can be found all over the global North, from the USA to Australia to continental Europe.

Ernesto and Celinda

Perhaps the best way of illustrating what goes on in an industry as fundamental to all of our daily needs as it is possible to be is through the testimony of two Bolivian workers, given just prior to their deportation from Britain. In the following paragraphs, we see how an enterprising couple sought to take their fate into their own hands in order to provide for their family. What happened was that their initiative was turned against them as they were plunged into a cesspit of exploitation.[45]

> We are Ernesto and Celinda, Bolivians from Cochabamba and we want to tell you our story and hope you understand us.
>
> In January [2005] we saw an ad in the paper saying you could work in England, earning £2,000 a month with accommodation, a visa and a secure job. I spoke with my wife and said we'd go to England, earn a little money to pay our debts and put some aside to buy a house.
>
> So we made contact with someone called Carolina, who assured us she had contacts with Portuguese people in England. She asked for $10,000, so my wife's brother got a loan from a moneylender at 3 per cent interest to be paid back in two to three months. We set off on 7 February and arrived in London that night. We were directed to a hotel where they told us to stay for two days – they'd said we wouldn't have to pay but we did.
>
> At this time we made contact with a Portuguese called Ailindo and his lover Sonia, a Bolivian. They took us to Brandon, a little

town outside Norwich, and we stayed in his house for two weeks and paid up the rest of the $10,000 cash. Then they took photos of us and I had to change my name to Ernesto da Silva Pereira. This Portuguese went off to London and the following day presented us with new identities and documents saying we were Portuguese.

Then they looked for work for us in Boston. One day they left us there working harvesting flowers for a Spaniard who worked and had an agency. He charged us two weeks' rent in advance and a deposit, some £300 in all. That's when I realised it was all a lie and I said as much to this Rafael the Spaniard. I said I didn't want to work and I wanted my money back, but he wouldn't return it.

The next day we went back to the house of the Portuguese man and said to him that we'd been lied to and wanted to go back to our country and get our money back. He said this wasn't possible because the money was already spent and we could do nothing because we were illegals, and what's more we had no proof. By now we were desperate for work and they sent us up to Scotland, to Aberdeen, to work in a fish-processing plant. There we were put up by his friend, another Portuguese, called Paulo, and his wife Maria. They charged us £100 each for finding the work.

We worked a couple of months there – April and May. They paid us £160 a week per person. This was paid into the account of the Portuguese couple because we had no account and from it they deducted rent of £50, £10 for transport and £40 for electricity and gas, council tax, water, TV and telephone. So they only actually gave us £50–£60 a week. What's more, there were eight people living in that house. In fact, we weren't earning any money – everything was for them. What's more, they had an agreement with the factory and denounced us as illegals, so we had to flee to London in early May and with what little money we had we rented a room for £140 for two weeks. We went off to another employment agency, one run by someone called Don Ricardo. He told us that in Leicester there was a fruit-salad factory that needed people to work in two shifts. We paid £200 each and set off for Leicester at the end of May. There we met another Portuguese, called Ubaldo, who was said to be from Mozambique and who took us on to work for June and part of July for an agency [name given] that operates in the city.

Each day we got up at 3.30 in the morning to take a bus to the city centre. From there we'd leave at 4.30 to arrive by 5.15 a.m. at the fruit-salad factory [name and location given], starting work at 5.30 and leaving at two in the afternoon, Monday to Friday. They paid us for just seven hours a day though.[Other days we'd work] until six in the evening. That's twelve hours but they only paid us for ten hours a day – £30 a day.

Then a number of Brazilians arrived so there were around 200 of us, illegals and others who were legal, including Indians, Iraqis and Poles.

We had to pay £3 a day for the bus and £5 a week to have our cheque cashed. Then each person paid rent. We were paying £40 a week and living thirteen people in one house.

On 20 July this Ubaldo told us we would have a visit at the factory from [a major high-street food retailer] and nobody should leave their place and we must behave well. We all believed this and on 22 July when everyone went to work – some 210 people – the three buses were stopped on the road by the police. They took us to a big police station in Leicester and there they began to separate the illegals from the legals, and the most curious thing was that all of the legals were carrying their passports that day and what's more the police had a list of everyone who was working and knew exactly who was legal and who was illegal. We were all agreed that the agency, through Ubaldo, had handed us over to Immigration to avoid a fine for the agency.

All the illegals were sent off to towns near Leicester. We were put in a cell without being fed and the next day sent to a detention centre.

This is the sad truth about what happened to us in Britain. On 3 August we'll leave with nothing. We've lost everything – our suitcases and two weeks' money the agency owes us. We don't have a cent to go home with. Worse, we know that we are going back to a debt that is growing. We can only pay the interest on the money we borrowed to come here and they've told us that my wife's brother's house that was put up as security is going to be taken. We are devastated and only God knows the Calvary we have lived here. In Bolivia we have two children, aged 6 and 3. We don't know how we'll feed and educate them. Then there are my younger brothers who I've been supporting through their studies.

That will have to change. We don't know what we are going to do. We leave here with no spirit, no possessions, no direction.

[Some of the details of this testimony, including names of people and companies, are supported by the separate testimony of one of the Brazilian workers referred to.]

The case of Ernesto and Celinda is not an isolated one. Across the global North, the rigours of just-in-time delivery, increased local and international competition, and the battle for profits between retail corporations has encouraged the flight of the local workforce from agriculture while sucking in migrant labour to fill the void. This is true in Greece and Spain, the USA and the UK. With these more recent developments coming on top of the natural seasonality of much agricultural work, the sector is one where labour providers – reputable and disreputable – flourish, where informal work is well established and where super-exploitation can be imposed easily. The location of many agricultural workplaces exacerbates the problem, adding geographical isolation to the linguistic problems workers face in securing their rights. The result is widespread abuse of workers that, at its worst, shades into bonded labour and other forms of forced labour – modern-day slavery in an industry on which every one of us depends everyday.

The Cleaning Industry

The cleaning industry in Britain had a turnover of some £9 billion a year in 2005, up from £5.3 billion in 1997 and with a projected growth rate of 12 per cent a year. Business is split 55:45 between the public sector and the private sector. The industry employs as many as 900,000 people. Some seventy companies account for 70 per cent of contract cleaning in the country.[46] The category of contract cleaning also includes recycling, building maintenance and renovation. Laundering and dry cleaning counted around 3,600 companies in 2002 with a turnover of £1.2 billion.[47]

Contract cleaning sounds like a healthy industry – large, a rapid rate of growth, somewhat concentrated but far from an oligopoly. However, profit margins are very slim, less than 4 per cent, and competition is intense. The sector has three main drivers at present: a shift away from simple cleaning and towards broader facilities management; continuing outsourcing of functions previously carried on in-house; and government bodies seeking to cut costs. The first of these is a reaction to the competitive pressure on margins; the second and third are strategies predicated on contractors doing the work cheaper than an in-house workforce. So, success in this highly labour-dependent sector is based largely on cost control and reduction. It is not surprising, then, that a high proportion of workers are migrants and that levels of pay are very low – even in London, just half the national average annual salary in 2005 for workers with the correct documentation.[48] Indeed some activists go further and say that not just low pay but abusive employment practices are systemic in the cleaning industry. Development of subcontracting and growth in the use of temporary labour, employment disguised as self-employment, and employment of undocumented workers have all been seen in the sector in France as well.[49]

Recruitment is largely through local advertising and word of mouth, although some in-house operations may use agencies. The HSE report found word of mouth to have been the most common route into a cleaning job. The very report on low-paid workers in London by Yara Evans that found that 90 per cent of low paid workers interviewed were migrants also discovered that some two-thirds of interviewees had found their job through a friend.[50] The Latin American Workers' Association in London agreed, saying jobs are generally found through the community when a migrant worker arrives, and adding that lack of language skills precludes going through agencies (while lack of legitimate documentation will rule out other routes).[51]

This lends geographical areas or business segments national or linguistic concentrations. This may provide an element of certainty of employment to newcomers but it can also trap particular nationalities or language groups into particular employment. The Queen Mary report noted that almost 60 per cent of cleaners on the London Underground were Nigerian or Ghanaian. Anglophone Africans were also the largest group in office cleaning, and in both segments Latin Americans were the second largest grouping. East Europeans and Asians were the most prominent groups in hotel cleaning.[52] The Latin American Workers' Association cited cleaning and catering as being the employment of arriving workers.

But, as with other sectors, the prominence of particular nationalities may change over time according to political and economic conditions in the countries of origin or to restrictions on entry. This may not be immediately apparent because of the prevalence of false passports on the one hand, and because of shared languages on the other. So, an employer may not spot the shifting pattern of Latin American nationals coming to him for jobs because they all speak Spanish or Portuguese and hold Iberian passports. And, after all, inasmuch as they are disposable, replaceable, undifferentiated, he does not care as long as they are functional.

The succession of one migratory group by another in the cleaning industry was recently documented in Spain too. There an established Ecuadorian, Filipino and Moroccan cleaning workforce is under pressure from an influx of Bolivians. The latter, it is reported, are generally undocumented and will (or have to) work for €4 an hour rather than the €8–10 an hour that the former, who generally have papers, could command.[53]

Hiring and firing and day-to-day control of work on site are generally the responsibility of a local manager or supervisor, who also has charge of wage sheets and attendance records.[54] Workers' representatives say it is very often at this level that abuse is orchestrated, with or without the knowledge, collusion, complicity or encouragement of head office. Contract cleaning workers often have insecure contracts and are frequently sacked for no obvious reason. The Latin American Workers' Association said workers are commonly sacked with the supervisor skimming the wage that is due. He also suspected that sometimes a worker will be fired but the name left on the books, so the ongoing wage payment from head office can be skimmed.

The person directly exploiting migrant workers is often a compatriot or, if not that, then someone with the same mother tongue. This has also been noted in other countries and other sectors with high migrant participation, including agriculture, food processing and the sex industry. The opportunity for someone with a command of both English and the language of the migrant to lever that advantage is obvious. Where jobs are made known by word of mouth, they can recruit. They can stand between employer and worker, broking, controlling and benefiting from the relationship. Interviews suggested this power position was as likely to be held by a woman as by a man.

They are also well placed to know and manipulate the fears of migrants. One case cited by a case worker in an interview for this book was that of a woman employed as a cleaner in the Houses of Parliament. She works four hours a day and her due pay is a paltry £400–500 a month, but half of that is skimmed by the Colombian supervisor who threatened to turn her in to the immigration authorities if she did not pay. This case is at the extreme end of the spectrum but that is not to say it is uncommon. The Latin American Workers' Association generally has some 200 cases pending. In May 2006, the Transport and General Workers' Union tried to intervene when six cleaning workers were apparently handed over to the immigration authorities by their employer, losing wages and possessions and, for some, contact with their children.[55] Public-sector Unison officials say they have heard of workers' passports being withheld and of threats to tip off immigration authorities.

Clearly systemic are low pay and poor conditions. The Queen Mary report found:

> 90 per cent of workers earning less than the Greater London Authority's Living Wage for London (£6.70 an hour). Average earnings were just £5.45 an hour.... This is less than half the national average salary and less than one third of average earnings in London.

The interviewees for the HSE report, which covered the country, not just London, were all earning the minimum wage or slightly above. A dry-cleaning worker said colleagues were still on the minimum wage three years after joining the company. Many contract cleaning staff work unsociable hours but receive no recognition of this. Piece rates are paid by some agencies supplying cleaners to hotels – £1.70 per room was cited by some Polish workers.[56] There is frequently no overtime rate, the studies found. Sick pay was received by only a minority of workers. Holiday entitlement tends to be the bare minimum.

These levels of pay leave people barely able to survive. A migrant cleaning worker at Whipps Cross Hospital in North-east London, earning £5.50 an hour for a 37-hour week, working for a high-street-name employment agency, with one child to support, had £45–50 in hand even after tax credits, having paid normal rent and utility bills and debt repayments of £40 a week.[57]

In some jobs with a high concentration of migrant workers, long hours are common. In contract cleaning this tends not to be the case. Indeed many workers are employed for just a few hours a day. This is probably one of the factors that genders the job – around two-thirds of workers in the sector are women and, as the Queen Mary study found, contrary to the stereotype of migrant workers being single, most live with family members.[58] The situation is different in laundering and dry cleaning. 'Adil Qusay lost his job when he began organising employees – mostly Polish and Pakistani – of American Dry Cleaners in North-west London. Most of the core workforce of around sixty in the cleaning plant were working 60–65 hours a week.[59]

It is scarcely surprising that staff turnover tends to be very high in cleaning jobs. This said, there is anecdotal evidence that trade union successes in raising the wage rate in North-east London hospitals for contracted cleaning staff has reduced turnover and may be a factor in limiting the penetration of accession-state citizens into this work.

Problems with language and fear are common among migrant workers, and no less in the cleaning sector than elsewhere. In some cases there are no contracts of employment. In others there is a contract but the worker signs away rights while in others the contract looks reasonable but is simply not adhered to. A worker who does not understand the contract he or she has signed is even less likely to have a grasp of the complexity of British immigration law. This can lead to workers fearing they have no right to be in the country when they do. Unison officials report cases of workers buying false documents when they had the legal right to work in Britain.

Fear of job loss and deportation and the impact that would have on families at home dependent on remitted wages makes organisation difficult. During attempts to organise at Whipps Cross Hospital a contractor suddenly demanded documentation from the workers, some of whom promptly disappeared. Going to employment tribunals is risky for irregular workers, whose status might emerge during proceedings, although the Latin American Workers' Association reported winning one such case for a cleaning worker.

Where health trusts have contracted out cleaning work, they have done so to cut costs. This has led to gross disparities between workers still employed directly and those working for contractors. A successful campaign in North-east London in 2006 to harmonise rates between NHS and contract cleaners, porters, domestics and others pushed rates up from around £5.50 an hour to £7–7.50. But, as a union official remarked, organising is not risk-free. Not only is there the danger of workers being intimidated by the contractor, there is also the risk that the NHS trust will acknowledge the situation and sack the contractor, resulting in the workers losing their jobs.

Cleaning, like agriculture, primarily demands unskilled workers, and so is not inherently choosy about their origins. That said, it is often marked by racial or linguistic factors for two apparent reasons. The first is that it is a sector that has been abandoned by indigenous workers because of its low pay and status, while simultaneously the rising employment levels of women in other occupations has fuelled demand. That demand is most easily met by incomers seeking a toehold in the local economy. Second, because migrants often do not have a good grasp of the local language or may not have access to formal routes to employment, word of mouth often determines recruitment. While this offers some advantages because individuals can secure leads for friends and relatives, it also opens up the possibility of a particular form of abuse where wage skimming and blackmail are carried out by earlier arrivals who have overcome language problems and established a relationship with the labour provider or employer.

Low wages are endemic to the industry and the global shift to subcontracting has extended the vulnerability of workers into areas such as work for municipalities or health authorities that used to maintain in-house workforces where unionisation was widespread. Working hours in the industry are frequently antisocial, with office blocks cleaned at night when cleaning will not disrupt other activity. And hours may not only be long and antisocial, they may also be short, requiring a worker to operate on more than one site in a single day.

The wage-skimming and the threats of deportation are clearly grossly abusive and, as in agriculture, allowing them to perpetuate amounts to turning a blind eye to forced labour.

Construction

> In nineteen hundred and eighty six
> There's not much for a chippie but swinging a pick
> And you can't live on love, on love alone
> So you sail cross the ocean, away cross the foam
> To where you're a Paddy, a Biddy or a Mick
> Good for nothing but stacking a brick
> Your best mate's a spade and he carries a hod
> Two work horses heavily shod.[60]

The lyrics of this twentieth-century Irish folk song could have been written in Spanish or Portuguese, Polish or Gujarati. More than half a million recently arrived, undocumented migrants work in the US construction industry, accounting for 5 per cent of the workforce. Longer-term undocumented labour accounts for another 7 per cent, taking the total to 1.4 million.[61] Some 7 per cent of documented migrant workers in Italy work in construction, ranging from a low of 2.8 per cent in the south to nearly 12 per cent in the north-west.[62] This is an industry that depends on overseas workers.

The construction industry employs between 2 and 2.5 million people in Britain, depending on which parameters are used to define a sector that runs from casual plastering in a house through to major national projects such as the benighted Wembley Stadium or the projected Crossrail link in London.

The big building and maintenance projects have always relied on transient labour supplying both skills and raw manpower. So, for example, power station maintenance has traditionally been carried out, on the one hand, by workers who live in a particular area because it affords easy access to several plants requiring regular work and, on the other, by groups of workers who travel from one end of the country to the other from contract to contract.

The canal and then the rail and road networks, palimpsests on which successive economic phases have depended, could only have been drawn across the landscape by itinerant labourers. The railway 'navvies' of the nineteenth century, originally sea wall builders from the fens and former canal diggers, moved like medieval armies from camp to camp with loose-knit families in tow. In 1845 there were 200,000 men building 3,000 miles of railway line.[63]

Irish labour was long an important part of the workforce, and its steady decline from the 1990s onwards marks an important cultural change in both Ireland and Britain. No longer will ballads of exile in London or Birmingham ring so true in Dublin or Cork. No longer will English children be told in the playground that the name of the housebuilder Wimpey is an acronym for 'We Import More Paddies Every Year'.

But if the national profile of the construction industry has altered, with an influx of southern European and then central European workers filling the vacuum left by the Irish exodus to a booming economy at home, the importance of a pool of temporary labour from the unskilled to the highly skilled has remained. In agriculture, the seasonality of harvest time is a major factor in demand for labour. It is also a factor in demand in construction in Britain but of far less importance. It does affect labour supply, as some central European workers will come to Britain when the more severe winters at home close the industry down. Construction and agriculture share the need for specific tasks to be carried out at a specific time – roofers or electricians must be available at the right moment in the project's progress, just as fruit pickers and packers must be ready as soon as the crop is ripe. For both industries place and time are immutable. Neither can relocate and both are time critical. This means there are also parallels in the structure of labour recruitment. Both require fast and flexible supply mechanisms. Agriculture makes extensive use of labour providers – gangmasters and others – where construction is characterised by subcontracting and self-employment (but also uses labour providers) so that a large site may employ workers from or through dozens of firms. Both systems, like others found in industries with large-scale migrant worker input, are susceptible to gross exploitation. Indeed, if abusive practices by gangmasters are squeezed out of the food industry, it is likely they will reappear in construction. In parts of Italy, the day market for North African and central European workers that occurs in agriculture is also common in construction, laying workers open to double exploitation by labour provider and employer.[64]

The number of migrant workers in the British construction industry cannot be judged with accuracy. The building workers' union Ucatt has estimated it at between 100,000 and 150,000.[65] The industry press tends to use a figure of 80,000.[66] While many of the incoming workers do unskilled or semi-skilled labouring work, the structure of the UK building industry has also created a need for skilled and specialist workers. Bricklayers are much in demand but may be recruited from almost any national group. But some skills are associated with particular nationalities. While the Irish veterans and the new recruits from the accession states are clearly the dominant nationalities among the non-British workforce in the sector, many others figure, including Indian, Brazilian, Jamaican, Chinese and Moroccan. Indeed, anecdotally, some employers are reputed to prefer non-EU migrants because they are more vulnerable. But the Portuguese are known for their concrete finishing and some south-east Europeans for specialist carpentry. Some central European workers have knowledge of techniques originally developed for cold climates.

Central European workers have become 'a functional substitute for departing Irish counterparts ... especially ... in those parts of the construction sector that are particularly prone to casualisation',[67] filling the vacancies for daywork and off-the-books labour as first- and second-generation Irish workers return to an Irish economy that for the first time in two centuries is importing rather than exporting workers. But the official figures for those coming in from the 2004 accession states are of little use except that they show a rising trend over three years of data. The total of 16,670 construction workers registering between accession and the end of June 2006 is just 4 per cent of the total under the scheme. However, it does not include all those describing themselves as self-employed and who do not need to register.

Structural labour shortage

The British construction industry suffers from chronic labour shortages that the departure of Irish workers has only exacerbated. The industry has been booming since the early 1990s with further growth in the pipeline, so demand for labour is increasing. The industry training body says 87,000 additional workers will be needed each year to 2010 with a swathe of projects in the south and east of England meaning employment growth rates there will be up to 18 per cent, while even in the north, where there will be a relative slowdown, the rate of increase will still be healthy.[68]

A series of high-profile projects around London has led to speculation that there will be a surge in the number of workers migrating to Britain to work on these sites. That is seen as unlikely in the industry. Work on the Olympics infrastructure will commence as work on Heathrow Terminal 5 comes to an end, and Crossrail will succeed the Olympics; the workforce will move from one to the next. However, these projects will bring opportunities for those with particular skills, such as the German workers on Terminal 5, and will exacerbate skills shortages in other parts of the country. The (probably significantly underestimated) annual inflow of foreign, skilled construction workers is forecast to slow somewhat to 3,150 over the next decade.[69]

Domestic supply has been shrinking. Ucatt says that much of this is due to the collapse of the apprenticeship system. Well over 90 per cent of companies employ fewer than twenty-five people and do not have training programmes. Only a quarter of companies that pay the training levy actually run training programmes. Meanwhile, over half of the skilled workforce is registered as self-employed because workers can reduce their tax bills while employers can hire and fire at will while not paying sick pay and holiday pay. There are particularly acute and abiding shortages of plasterers, carpenters and bricklayers. A consequence of the labour shortage has been an increase in wages over the past twenty years. A study by Deloitte for the government said they had risen by a factor of 3.5 in the period, averaging 6.5 per cent a year (but slowing in more recent years), while prices charged by construction companies had not kept pace.[70] This means that labour costs – always accounting for a large proportion of the total in construction – have become increasingly important in costing work. That, of course, gives employers an incentive to find ways of reducing the wage bill.

There is, then, a twofold employer demand for migrant labour in the sector: meeting a skills shortage; and suppressing the generalised rise in wages. The two are inter-related, of course. Local workers with skills that are in short supply can demand higher remuneration, although incomers with less market intelligence are less likely to do so, particularly if they are being paid more than they would be at home due to macroeconomic factors. So, highly skilled Romanian carpenters were employed to do panelling on the Scottish Parliament building at rates substantially lower than local workers could have commanded. The contractor's excuse was that there was no suitable labour available in the Edinburgh area.

In early 2004, a group of unions published a pamphlet condemning energy group RWE for contracting out engineering construction work to low paid Portuguese migrant workers, a practice the unions termed 'social dumping'.[71] According to a union official, the use of imported workers at one north Midlands power station caused resentment among the established workforce that was fostered by lack of a common language and by employer attempts to keep the groups of workers separate, so while the migrant workers were in fact being paid low rates and required to work long hours, the British workforce assumed the migrants were being paid the going rate and snapping up all the available overtime work.

Ucatt says there is evidence that employers are using migrant workers to erode national pay scales. In 2006, the agreed rate for a bricklayer was over £9 an hour but the union says that migrants employed through agencies are being paid less. An excellent report on the situation in north-east England found one Polish bricklayer who had been promised the national rate but was actually being paid a piece rate that he did not know while others were being paid well under £5 an hour.[72] Bricklayers have skills that are in high demand in Britain and yet could still be paid under half the agreed rate. For general labourers, for whom the national rate at the time was £6.77 an hour, the same report found actual hourly rates of £1.92 and £2.44.

In September 2006, the industry press reported that a member of parliament for Southampton, where some 10 per cent of the workforce is Polish, had written to the prime minister expressing his concern that the day rate for building workers had fallen by 50 per cent to just £60 a day since accession. The same report quoted a Ucatt regional official, saying migrant workers were being paid only 60 to 80 per cent of the local going rate.[73]

Some agencies are explicit in their marketing. A report written for the Trades Union Congress cited one saying its services could help 'bring their [skilled workers'] present excessive labour rates to a more acceptable commercial level'.[74] Another promises that productivity can be boosted by 25 per cent by bringing in central European workers.

Evidence that migrant labour is being used to undercut local wages rates comes not only from the labour movement. The Deloitte report links the slowdown in wage rises for skilled workers in the sector to increased migration, saying:

> the influx of accession state EU workers has had a balancing impact.... Over the last five years, the average increase in wages for skilled workers has been 4.4 per cent per annum, identical to average wage inflation for the economy as a whole. Moreover, wage inflation for unskilled workers in the construction industry has been just 3.9 per cent.[75]

Looking ahead, the same report expects continued inward migration to be a factor in slowing wage growth in coming years. In the autumn of 2006, the industry's training body opened an office in Poland to fast-track workers to Britain.[76]

The abuse of labour: from the Lump to Losc

The innumerable small sites and the vast number of small firms and self-employed workers means that much building work is scarcely policed or monitored for health and safety let alone for employment practices. On big projects the household-name company whose advertising hoardings surround the site will have little if anything to do with labour recruitment, which takes place through subcontracts that can spin a spider's web of agreements with smaller contractors, agencies, gangmasters and sole traders. This is known as 'labour only sub-contracting' (Losc) and means, 'while the number of workers employed on a construction site may be large, the actual number on the books of the main builders may be very small'.[77] A migrant worker may be employed directly by a building company, through an agency, or individually if he holds the easy-to-obtain Inland Revenue self-employed card. The industry has a history of fly-by-night agencies that disappear, owing workers their wages, and labour provision in the industry has always had its murky side, so it is not surprising that there are tales of gangs instructing subcontractors who they should take on. The Transport and General Workers' Union, with support of others in the industry, has called for the extension of legislation covering gangmastering in the food industry to the construction sector.

The prevalence of self-employment and off-the-books working that has characterised the British industry since the infamous days of the Lump in the 1970s encourages a casualisation of the migrant workforce. In the late 1990s, *Building Magazine* ran an exposé of the 'dawn trade' in Albanian, Kosovan and Ukrainian labour in North London. A few years on, in areas of West London with large migrant worker concentrations (sometimes grafted on to long-established Polish communities), it is Polish workers who advertise in newsagent windows and wait around at six in the morning in the hope of a van arriving to pick up workers for the day. These more recent human waves are the reinforcements to the ranks of construction's reserve army of labour, depleted by the return home of so many of the Irish rank and file as the 'Celtic Tiger' economy boomed.

Manipulation of employment status is found elsewhere. Austria has experienced the growth of pseudo-self-employment in construction since the 2004 accession, running alongside pseudo-companies that fold before the tax bill arrives, costing the government billions of euros each year.[78] In Italy, incomers are increasingly involved in the subcontracting of work to false co-operatives, the members of which are registered as self-employed.[79]

Along with the plethora of workplaces and of suppliers of labour, plus the time-limited nature of the work, the construction industry has a number of reported similarities of forms of exploitation in common with agriculture.

The north-east England report found instances of poor quality tied accommodation with rent deducted from wages. Weekly deductions of as much as £30 for transport were recorded. The majority of workers were found not to have employment contracts or to have contracts that bore little relation to the reality. Payslips were often wrong or simply not issued. Some employers deducted tax and national insurance but would not confirm employment so workers could get National Insurance cards. In effect this practice ties the worker to the employer unless the former is willing to work elsewhere illegally or fraudulently obtain a card (available for around £70 on the black market). Travel and holiday allowances were frequently not paid. Many were working long hours even if they had not signed Working Time Directive waivers, and some were allotted unpaid duties.[80] In other words, many of the conditions found in the food sector and the cleaning industry are found in construction.

Attempts to resist such conditions have resulted in violence against workers and threats against union officials. The same report details several accounts, including one that led to strike action by

Polish workers. In their paper on forced labour in Britain, Andersen and Rogaly cite two Polish construction workers who were badly beaten after being moved from workplace to workplace, closely monitored and not paid.[81] Another case of the use of forced labour made the headlines because the employer was a former senior executive of Barclays Bank and founder of his own church. Pieter van Rooyen was jailed for three months in 2006 for providing false documents to bring five South African labourers to the Isle of Man to renovate his house. They were paid £1.36 an hour for a 72-hour week for some of the period and prevented from leaving the property.[82] The opening of the new temple in Wembley in North-west London was rightly celebrated as an achievement of the Hindu community there, but the building of the temple had stirred controversy for the treatment of highly specialised artisans brought in from India. Stone masons were paid just 30 pence an hour while living in a shack on the site. They had been employed through a company in India and then seconded to a sister company involved in the work in England.[83]

Again, abuses found in Britain are mirrored elsewhere. In Norway a series of site visits by the Labour Inspection Authority found 'that many employees are being paid substantially less than is obligatory under collective agreements. Moreover, these employees work under hazardous work environment conditions and are often subject to appalling living conditions.'[84] The same report noted that lack of resources meant that many cases of illegally low payment were never followed up by the police. In Austria, the 'posted worker' arrangement has been abused in the sector. Under the scheme, foreign workers may be seconded from a foreign company by a local employer for a period of up to six months. Austria's work conditions and pay levels are supposed to be observed. But in one publicised case an industrial construction and demolition company brought in 150 workers from South

Korea and Indonesia. They were found to be working up to 62 hours a week at little more than one-tenth of the official rate for the job.[85] In Ireland, Turkish-owned Gama Construction, which then employed 800 migrants in the country, was accused in April 2005 of underpaying its Turkish workers posted to Ireland. While Gama paid its Irish workers €13 an hour, its Turkish workers received a small stipend in Ireland with the rest of their wages paid to accounts in the Netherlands that the workers said they were unaware of and could not access.[86]

Turning a blind eye

Clearly, as with other industries that make extensive use of migrant labour, the construction industry throws up cases of extreme abuse that can legitimately be labelled 'forced labour' in accordance with the conventions of the UN's International Labour Organisation. Building workers do, on occasion, face threats and physical harm, withholding of wages, retention of passports and other indicators of forced labour. While extreme, such conditions are not on a different plane from those faced by a far greater number of workers in the sector; rather, they are at the far end of a continuum that is predicated on increasing profit margins by squeezing labour costs. To split off the most dramatic cases risks falling into the government position of hiving off a few 'law and order', 'victims and villains' cases while tacitly condoning more widespread exploitation.

And it is easy to draw the conclusion that collusion is exactly the approach of government. The fragmented structure of the construction industry encourages recruitment that is difficult to monitor and even more difficult to police. The labour is temporary, record-keeping is bad, false documentation easy to obtain and checks infrequent. In a period when employers have the incentive and the opportunity to drive down labour costs and fill skills gaps through the use of migrants, they will do so if they can. However, there is the suspicion that the agencies charged with controlling the industry are not only overstretched and under-resourced but leak information to those they are supposed to be policing. A Ucatt official goes so far as saying that raids on sites by the Health and Safety Executive, the Home Office, the Inland Revenue and so on are generally leaked beforehand so undocumented workers and those working off the books do not turn up for a day or two.

The same suspicion abides in independent studies:

> The problems of enforcing regulations in the construction sector, combined with a lack of policing, suggests that the authorities turn a blind eye to foreign workers in the construction sector and that the dynamics of this particular sector open small doors for the employment of regular and irregular migrant workers beyond the prying eyes of the state.[87]

And back in late 2001, the influential *Building Magazine* ran an investigation into the use of irregular foreign labour on British building sites.[88] From the start it depicted the issue in xenophobic terms, accusing the government of failing in a promise to 'clamp down' on 'illegal immigrants'. But, on the basis of good knowledge of the sector and a number of interviews, it concluded that the government was deliberately avoiding the issue and making little or no effort to crack down on large-scale employment of irregular workers or to recoup billions of pounds in consequent lost revenues. Some of its interviewees said the government ignored the matter because to do otherwise would be too costly to the industry and would also push up the price of government building contracts.

To limit debate within the confines of a popular panic over immigration misses the more fundamental point that use of migrant labour is part of the very structure of the construction industry not only in Britain but in many other countries as diverse as

Austria and Dubai. But this may not have been so apparent in 2001, well before the ordered influx of 2004 accession-state workers re-emphasised that migrant labour does not have to be 'irregular', 'illegal', 'undocumented' for it to entail exploitation over and above that which the local workforce would accept.

Land, Sea and Airports

The use of migrant labour changes and expands constantly. Recent years have seen the development of a hand car-washing industry operating from small plots of urban space and from municipal and supermarket car parks. There is anecdotal evidence that many of these operations are staffed by migrant workers, many of them 'irregular'. In October 2006, the trade press drew attention to the growing use of migrant workers to fill 'some of the less glamorous non-skilled roles' in the printing industry.[89]

The security industry, despite recent attempts to clean up its image and introduce a licensing regime, is developing a reputation for using and abusing migrant labour. A Nigerian who arrived in Britain in 2003 and lived in Manchester, and was set to be deported in the autumn of 2006, detailed (with names and addresses) how he had been taken on by a small security firm in Manchester that had been contracted by a larger company with operations throughout Britain and in continental Europe. No identification or documentation was requested. After two weeks, the worker was paid cash in hand. But then he (and a number of other irregular migrants) worked for six weeks without receiving £1,270 owed to him, the subcontractor telling the workers that the cheque from the bigger company had bounced. When he persisted in asking about the money he was told to bring in his National Insurance card. A few days later he was picked up on the street by the police.[90]

Migrant workers have been employed for some time at British airports to carry out service jobs such as baggage handling. The GMB union has had an agreement with Swissport, a major international airport service company, whereby workers are employed directly after three months of satisfactory work through an agency. But in October 2006 organiser Gary Pearce discovered that the agency had begun to supply 'self-employed' Polish workers at Stansted airport in Essex. Initially a group of around twenty, but with more being recruited, these workers were supplied through Labour Source in East London, said the GMB, put into accommodation by an associated company, and registered as self-employed and administered through a third. Labour Source would have gained by not having to pay National Insurance contributions for them, and their status would mean they were not entitled to sick pay or holiday pay.

The union said the workers were being charged a sizeable up-front rental charge that they would forfeit if they left the accommodation during the six-month contract period, as well as a deposit and an agency fee of £250. They were left with around £250 a month for food and personal expenses after bills, said Gary Pearce. The agency denied that accommodation was overcrowded, but the GMB said living rooms were being used for sleeping.

In the galleys

The Trades Union Congress has called on the British government to amend the Race Relations Act in a bid to stop blatant and entirely legal discrimination against foreign seafarers working for British employers. The TUC said the practice was widespread and argued:

> it is simply not acceptable that Indian, Polish, Portuguese or other migrant workers can be paid lower rates on British ships than

their colleagues who are British nationals. It leads shipowners to try and sack their workforces and replace them with workers of different nationalities at lower rates.[91]

The TUC demand was prompted by a bitter dispute involving the company Irish Ferries, a dispute that generated much anger on both sides of the Irish Sea. In late 2005 Irish Ferries announced plans to slash its wage bill by 20 per cent, some €11 million a year. It would switch from direct employment of seafarers to agency crewing and, as it transpired, the majority of the crews would be eastern Europeans. The company cited higher fuel costs, the advent of low air fare travel and new ferry competitors using agency crews as the reasons for the restructuring.[92] Eventually, 90 per cent of the directly employed crew – some 500 workers – took redundancy. But before this, two ferries were occupied for several weeks by crew members after company security men tried to take over the vessels and bring on agency staff said to be paid just £2.60 an hour.[93]

Just a year later another dispute erupted around a vessel working the Irish Sea. This time the vessel involved was Jamaican flagged and operated by a subsidiary of Danish shipowner Maersk, while the crew members were Polish, Ukrainian and Russian. Union officials found one one able seaman who should have been earning around $3,200 a month, in accordance with his first contract of employment, was only being paid around $1,000 for 365-plus hours a month – or just over €2 an hour – on a second contract of employment. Another crew member who should have been earning $1,984 was being paid only $850.[94] Such disputes serve to illustrate that exploitative labour practices at sea are part and parcel of the way some companies operating within European waters do their business.

The shipping industry is rife with extreme exploitation and, indeed, forced labour. By its nature the industry is international, and shipowners have been able to use this to their advantage. A vessel may be owned in one country, 'flagged' in another, operated by a company in a third country, and crewed by an agency based in a fourth using seafarers from a number of countries. It may then ply its trade between a whole different set of countries. This makes the enforcement of minimum labour standards a challenge.

The 'flag of convenience' system allows a vessel to join, for a fee, the registry of one of the group of countries that earn substantial revenues from their 'flag'. The maritime laws of that country then apply to the vessel and to its crew. Needless to say, the attraction is that regulation is laxer and invites abuse. Crew members are subject to the labour laws of the flag nation. Many 'flag of convenience' vessels are in a parlous condition and the number of losses is high.

The International Transport Workers' Federation is a grouping of some 600 trade unions across the globe; its inspectors have spent decades documenting and combating the abuses that take place at sea. Among the most dramatic is the abandonment of crews by shipowners rather than paying them. In a report to the UN,[95] the ITF identified eighteen current cases of abandonment. One such case was the *Al Manara*, whose twenty crew members from India, Burma, Somalia, Iraq, Ukraine, Sudan and Ethiopia were abandoned in the Seychelles unpaid after seven months' work, during which they were shot at by armed guards on the ship. There are documented cases of seafarers not being paid for years. The crew of the oil tanker *Capbreton 1* stayed with the vessel when its French owner sold it to a Nigerian company. Not only were they not paid, they suffered lack of food and water. The vessel was then accused of carrying stolen oil, and the crew – all from West African countries – were held in jail for twenty-one months as if they were the criminals.

In each of five years covered in the report, the ITF encountered between 702 and 811 cases of wages being owed. The number of abandoned crews ranged from 19 a year to 44. On top of that were hundreds of instances of substandard food and accommodation, lack of safety, imposition of agency fees, and victimisation.

For millions of well-heeled Europeans and North Americans, the direct contact they have with seafarers is limited to the crew of cruise liners, a booming business sector. Behind the smart uniforms and professional smiles of the workers, there often lies a story of gross exploitation, even for those working for the key industry players such as Carnival and P&O Princess. For staff such as waitresses, salaries as low as $45 a month have been found, justified by the possibility of winning tips.[96] Seven days a week, and ten or twelve or even fourteen hours a day working is common for low wages. Many workers taken on are charged exorbitant agency fees that, in effect, turn them into bonded labourers. Fees of $1,500–$2,000 were found to be paid by workers from the Philippines, India and Indonesia. That money is usually borrowed from family members. Typically, the ITF says, over the period of a contract, a seafarer on a cruise liner will spend the first few months paying off these costs, then remit around $300 a month for three or four months, before being laid off for several months, all in all amounting to earnings of only around $100 a month. Arbitrary dismissals, sexual exploitation, and division of labour along racial grounds are also reported to be common.

North Sea labour crisis

The North Sea oil and gas industry has a staffing crisis that runs from highly specialised engineers through to platform workers such as riggers and catering staff. This is a result of an exodus from the industry during periods of low oil prices that, along with the depletion of more easily accessible reserves, meant less exploration and development work being carried out in the relatively high-cost North Sea. During that downturn the industry failed to recruit and train new staff. The numbers employed fell by around a third to 270,000 between 1997 and 2001. When oil prices recovered from the Southeast Asia economic crisis of the late 1990s and then roared ahead as Chinese and Indian demand burgeoned and supply was constrained due to disastrous US and British adventurism in the Middle East, oil companies were once more interested in the North Sea. But by this point the average offshore worker was in his late forties, only half of the specialist engineering students in the country were domestic students, and lack of apprenticeships and requirements to pay for their own compulsory survival training were putting off young people.

In 2006 the sector skills council for the oil industry was scrambling to introduce a programme to reverse a decline that meant the North Sea was reckoned to be short of 150 riggers as it approached the summer platform maintenance period. Recruitment of overseas engineers was quickly suggested. The oil industry is multinational and British staff have always been posted to all corners of the globe by the likes of BP and Shell and the big contractors, or have gone to work for US corporations. Now industry executives are advocating hiring engineering graduates from China, India, the former Soviet Union, Brazil and elsewhere to fill a skills gap created by the lack of indigenous job candidates.[97]

In 2005, the Offshore Industry Liaison Committee (OILC), an outspoken trade union for upstream oil workers, drew attention to the use of cheap, migrant workers offshore. Brought in by agencies, the workers originated from Portugal, Lithuania, Poland and the Philippines. A contract for a Maltese painter stipulated the worker would have to repay all or part of his training expenses if he failed to carry out ten assignment periods offshore. He would also be responsible for the costs of a replacement if he was absent. He was also legally bound to accept an assignment, while the agent 'is under no obligation to employ the services of the contractor [worker]' and 'is not to be considered as obliged to provide to the contractor any given amount of work per day or per week or per month'. Furthermore, the worker is excluded from holiday pay, including for statutory holidays, from sick pay and from pension payments. The daily wage for this amounted to around £45.[98]

The following year offshore contractor Amec announced it would use overseas labour in its North Sea operations to complement recruitment and training initiatives in Britain and to help it over a bulge of work on the Buzzard, Armada and Britannia fields. It brought in between 200 and 300 Filippino workers. Amicus and the GMB, both of which have sizeable memberships offshore, said they were concerned this would lead to the introduction of cheap labour, undercutting local workers and undermining agreed pay scales. The company and the two unions met and reached an agreement that Alan Harvey, the Amicus national organiser, described as 'a step in the right direction'.[99] The deal said that any imported workers would have to be competent, be able to communicate in English well enough to comply with safety standards, and would be paid the agreed industry rate for the job and have their expenses paid as per the industry norm.

But this 'positive development' quickly came under fire from the OILC (which has always accused its larger peers of selling their members short). Its general secretary, Jake Molloy, pointed to a key part of the agreement that said: 'Amec give a commitment that in any down-manning situation sub-contracted personnel will be prioritised before direct employees.' This, said the OILC, was clearly discriminatory and a jettisoning of integrity. It also challenged the safety situation where migrant workers were being used on two installations. The Health and Safety Executive wrote back saying: 'Our initial findings are that your concerns appear to be justified. In particular, Amec and Nexen have failed to demonstrate the competency of riggers on the [Buzzard] project. Other trades are being reviewed.'[100]

At the same time, the OILC suspected that other parts of the agreement were not being adhered to. Jake Molloy said members of the OILC had been told by Filippino workers that they were being paid $10.60 an hour where the agreed rate was £14.50 (around $27). He also said he was not convinced they were spending as much time as they should onshore between assignments but that this was difficult to monitor because the Filippino workers were not obliged to carry the Offshore Passports used by local workers to record medical history, time off, safety qualifications and so on.[101] Despite the assurance from Amec that the use of migrant labour was temporary, the OILC believes more and more overseas labour is being brought into the North Sea because it is cheaper than training and paying local workers.

The beauty of easier and cheaper international travel for employers is that labour mobility is increased so gaps in the workforce can be plugged quickly and inexpensively, compensating for the unforeseen. The lack of forethought by the oil industry can be rectified by the importation of Russian engineers or Maltese painters. An inadequate supply of bus drivers, satisfied in the 1950s by West Indian immigrants, can be bolstered with Poles and Turks. Seafaring is one of the most internationalised occupations that exists, but, as the Irish Ferries dispute underlined, where there was an opportunity to extend it further and increase margins through the wholesale replacement of one workforce with a cheaper, foreign one, there was an employer willing to do it. And, again, the exploitation of migrant workers over and above the exploitation of indigenous workers is seen to be all around us and integral to our own movement around the world.

Hospitality

The hospitality sector employs almost 2 million people in Britain across a diverse range of businesses from the school canteen to the five-star hotel, travel agents to Chinese restaurants, pubs and bars to restored steam railways. This is part of the secular rise of the service economy in the global North. In the UK, between 1999 and the second quarter of 2006, the number of manufacturing jobs fell from almost 4 million to under 3 million while the number of service jobs rose from under 19 million to over 21.5 million.[102]

The very breadth of the industry means the challenges facing the proprietor of one enterprise can be very different from those facing another. Many restaurants, for example, noticed a drop-off in custom when pub licensing hours were extended, and habitually see a dip during major sporting competitions such as the World Cup. Tourist attractions and hotels may be affected by events such as the London Tube bombings of 2005, foot-and-mouth disease or avian flu, which reduce tourists' propensity to travel. But, as a whole, the sector faces low productivity and labour shortages and uses large numbers of migrant workers. The industry's skills council puts the proportion of workers from overseas at 17 per cent.[103] In Spain, non-Spanish workers account for around 13 per cent of hotel and catering staff.[104]

But in Britain the raw figures disguise extreme concentrations, as for example in ethnic cuisine restaurants. There is also geographical concentration, with migrants most often found in London and other tourist destinations such as Edinburgh. Asked to approximate the proportion of migrant labour in their workforce, managers of twenty-five of London's top hotels came up with 70 per cent.[105]

Increased consumer choice in rich countries concatenates competition within the sector. Lower airline ticket prices to an increasing number of destinations mean the well-heeled now compare the price and attractiveness of a weekend in Norfolk with a weekend in Prague, or the cost of a train ticket from London to Scotland with one from London to Paris. A generation ago British holidaymakers were getting used to choosing between Cornwall and Corfu. Now they are used to considering Florida or Cancún. In the face of that competition, the low productivity of the British hospitality sector when compared with other sectors and with its peers overseas matters. On the high street, food outlets have proliferated, so long-established local Indian and Chinese restaurants are likely to compete with several similar rivals and a host of Italian and Thai eateries, themed chains with a continental sound to the name, pub food, and takeaways.

Labour shortage is endemic and turnover is exceptionally high. Some 40 per cent of jobs are classified as hard to fill and annual turnover of staff is 30 per cent. That means some 600,000 people leave a job in the sector each year (although many may go straight to another post in the industry). At the same time, demand for labour is expanding. But what is perhaps the most surprising finding is that only 14 per cent of employers felt that turnover was too high.[106] That suggests that many view their workers as commoditised and undifferentiated. Such a view can only be encouraged by the high proportion – some 50 per cent – of jobs that are described as requiring low skill levels. Fluctuations in demand for services – hourly in a pub or restaurant, perhaps daily for a contract caterer, and seasonal for hotels and tourist attractions – lead to a high level of part-time and temporary working. Academics looking at the industry ponder the advantages of just-in-time labour supply through agencies. Business software manufacturers promote tools to enable:

> A gradual move from inflexible/fixed contracts to more effective flexible agreements that better suit the demands of customers;

an optimised full time/part time mix across the seasons of the year; the design of optimal rosters to recruit for new openings or departmental re-organisations; more effective exceptional demand planning such as peak period temporary staff recruitment at Christmas.[107]

The restaurant segment of the industry is the biggest employer, accounting for well over one-quarter of all workers and around one-third of establishments.[108] Given that a high proportion of restaurants and takeaway food businesses offer food associated with the Indian subcontinent or China, it is not surprising that the largest category of workers from overseas (prior to the wave of new accessions to the EU, at any rate) was from Asia and the Middle East.

The use of migrant labour by ethnic cuisine restaurants is more complex than that of, say, hotels. Tokens of perceived ethnicity are core to the offering, even if the perception is replete with misnomers, myths and locally generated expectations. For example: 'Indian' restaurants are, by and large, Bangladeshi; the dishes served often bear little resemblance to anything eaten in the country of origin – indeed the famous balti dish, according to urban myth at any rate, emerged from Kashmiri eateries in the Ladypool Road in south Birmingham in the early 1980s; the decor of a standard high-street Indian restaurant is standardised, sometimes to the point of parody. A major part of the package is the ethnicity of the staff. An Indian restaurant must be seen to have staff who derive from the subcontinent. An Indian restaurant could no more be staffed by Polish workers than a Chinese restaurant could be staffed by Bangladeshis.

In Spain also, where hotel and catering jobs tend to be transitional for non-national labour – between first entry jobs in domestic services or construction and for the fortunate a move into better-paid work – ethnicity often determines employment as it does in contract cleaning work in the UK. Customer-facing tasks tend to be awarded to Latin American and Filipino migrants but other groups will often gravitate towards enterprises that only employ from particular ethnic backgrounds such as Turkish, Arab, or Chinese restaurants.[109]

But generational change has brought a labour crisis in ethnic catering in Britain. For most family-owned high street restaurants, opening hours are long and anti-social, margins are low, many of the jobs are unrewarding and the wages are very poor, and competition is cut throat. Members of the younger generations frequently want to escape the trade rather than continue it. That leaves an ageing generation of founders in search of cheap labour of the same ethnicity. Some of that labour can be unskilled, but availability of good chefs is very tight. The 9,500 Indian restaurants have to find 20,000 new workers each year.[110] Migrant labour, frequently undocumented, sometimes with a kinship to the owner, fills the gap. A Chinese community activist goes so far as to say that the Chinese catering industry would simply collapse without the inflow of undocumented workers who arrive in London and then find jobs with low pay and poor conditions in kitchens all over the country.[111] The experience of the Turkish and Kurdish communities in London has been different. Changes to international tariff rules for clothing almost destroyed the sweatshop industry in North London, which was a major employer for the communities. Capital that was not transferred abroad was ploughed into retail and catering, taking many younger family members with it.[112]

Monder Ram, Paul Edwards and Trevor Jones have undertaken detailed research on the use of undocumented workers in Indian restaurants and, later, on (non-)compliance with the minimum-wage legislation. They interviewed owners and workers, finding most workers to have migrated for primarily economic reasons although some had political reasons. Most entered the country illegally in lorries and most had paid for an agency or smuggling operation to get them to Britain. The journeys were usually financed by family and seemed to take two or three years to pay off (this chimes with cases quoted by Chinese activists). The undocumented workers complained they were at the bottom of the pile at the workplace.[113] Patronage may provide the job and some form of accommodation but it also leaves the workers open to demands that they work longer and for less than others. One said the owner had refused to hand over money he had been saving towards repayment of his debts.

Wage rates were extremely low. Most establishments studied breached minimum wage levels, with workers being required to be at their jobs for whatever hours the owner required. Recent arrivals working as kitchen porters were being paid no more than £2 an hour for a 50-hour week.[114] A later study, which took in all workers, found a majority of establishments requiring 45 to 50 hours a week and average wages of just £3–4 an hour, and the lowest paid (likely to be undocumented workers) still earning as little as £2.20 an hour.[115] Many workers also received well under the minimum legal holiday entitlement. Evasion of the minimum wage appeared to be easy, with the books showing fewer workers than were actually employed or by declaring that no one worked more than eight hours a day.[116] This evidence accords with that given by activists in the Latin American community in London, who say workers are sometimes paid just £2 an hour. Chinese workers have been known to be paid as little as £2 a day, with their accommodation comprising a mattress on the kitchen floor, say community workers.

The Citizens' Advice Bureau lists the hospitality sector as one that throws up cases of exploitation of migrant workers. It has cited a chef in a Thai restaurant with a work permit earning £2.50 an hour for a 60-hour week, no statutory sick pay, and half his holiday entitlement; a Ukrainian couple working for a national restaurant chain for four years without any paid holiday; and Spanish hotel workers earning less than the minimum wage.[117] The CAB also identified as a relatively new phenomenon the recruitment abroad of motorway service station staff by agencies and gangmasters. Most are used as cleaners but some work in kitchens. Abuses included deduction of £200 a month from total wages of £600 a month for provision of accommodation, and non-provision of pay slips, contract or national insurance number.[118]

An Anti-Slavery International researcher reported a case that clearly qualified as forced labour. Two Vietnamese workers were promised jobs in a hotel in Britain. They paid £18,000 to an agent to get into the country. On arrival, the person who met them took away their passports. They worked at a hotel owned by a major international chain for two months without pay. When they refused to work, their families in Vietnam received threats.[119] Elsewhere, a Polish hotel worker reports seeing a group of replacement workers sitting in an agent's car while he and his colleagues were being detained by immigration officials he believes were summoned by his employer to avoid paying wages.[120]

The pattern is becoming familiar. Migrant workers in the hospitality sector are being underpaid and having extra hours squeezed out of them, just as occurs in agriculture or construction. And wheeling around them are the vultures demanding high rents for poor accommodation, charges for minor administrative services, commission for finding work. Again, in extreme cases, there is coercion and manipulation of immigration status, used as means of controlling and disposing of people. Undoubtedly there are malign and unscrupulous individuals involved in the abuse of workers in the hospitality sector. It would be difficult not to impugn the character of someone prepared to threaten another person with deportation if they did not submit to control, or someone who knowingly reduced a worker's income to a pittance through excessive deductions.

The morality is more nuanced when we look at the high street restaurant struggling to survive a flood of competition, needing to replace cheap labour of the son or daughter with no interest in the family business. Here the relationships become more personal and more complex. The workforce is small, the workplace intimate. The worker may live with the owner's family. Patronage rather than cold impersonality determines the relationship, yet still the worker is undeniably being grossly overworked and underpaid. It is here, where we may sympathise with the plight of the employer as well as the worker, that the structural impetus towards the abuse of migrant labour is most clear. It is a matter of survival for the restaurateur, just as the farmer may claim the supermarket squeezes his margins. But then the director of a hotel chain would probably argue the same case faced with competition from other chains, other regions, other countries.

Domestic Labour

The domestic labour sector is a mess of ambiguities, elisions and ill-fitting definitions. These stem largely from the relationship between worker and employer, which remains a potent mix of power and intimacy, an exaggerated version of the interplay between the struggling restaurant owner and his migrant workers.

Domestic labour is heavily gendered – though perhaps not to the extent one would imagine. It may be racialised as well, even beyond many employers' preference for a foreign national. This section is concerned primarily with some of the most vulnerable domestic workers, migrants tied to direct, full-time employment with a single employer, usually resident in the employer's household. In the global North, demand for domestic labour, temporary and permanent, full-time and part-time, live-in and live-out is on an upward trend. This is driven by women's increased participation in the workforce, less reliance on other family members for help, and an ageing population. Though the focus here is on rich countries, this is work that spans time and place. India recently introduced a ban on the use of children as domestic labourers. Human Rights Watch has detailed gross abuse of child workers as young as 5 years old in Morocco[121] and the high incidence of workplace accidents and suicides among migrant domestic workers in Singapore.[122]

Just as many migrant workers in agriculture or construction or hospitality are perfectly happy with their arrangements, so it is fair to assume that there are many migrant women working as maids-cum-nannies-cum-carers in satisfactory circumstances. But the evidence is that a large number confront abysmal working hours and pay. On top of that, their location, hidden within the employer's household, leaves them prey to emotional manipulation, physical abuse and sexual exploitation. Bridget Anderson's book *Doing the Dirty Work* is a valuable investigation and analysis of the industry. She comments that, 'The difficulty for the worker is that, as 'domestic worker' is a role, living in she has no rest from that role but is living it twenty-four hours a day. It is as if the employer is buying not just her time but her very self'[123] and that: 'The clearest example of this is the many arguments live-in workers have with employers over food, surely one of the most basic human requirement. Baths, sleeping arrangements, letters from home, clothes worn – there is no aspect of the live-in worker's life that cannot be scrutinised by the employer.'[124] The degree of control is that much greater when the worker is a child.

Domestic work in general can provide a path towards integration into the broader host economy. So, in Spain where more than half of the domestic labour workforce is from overseas, undocumented migrant workers can gain residence rights if they can prove they have legal employment, but the employer has the advantage that the worker's immigration status means they may have to accept low pay. Indeed, the influx of migrant domestic workers saw pay rates for live-in workers decline from €600–720 a month to €360–540 in 2002.[125] Domestic work accounts for nearly 50 per cent of the migrant workforce in Spain, employing almost 400,000 workers in 2005, 90 per cent of them women, mostly from South America but with growing numbers from central Europe.[126] For most of the workforce, the work is not bound to one employer or to live-in employment but to a number of short jobs per day or week for various employers. For these workers, a major problem can be working enough hours to qualify for the social security system. Of the total number of domestic workers in Spain, some 6 per cent (around 24,000) live in, although 24 per cent (nearly 100,000) work for just one employer.

In Italy at the beginning of the decade domestic work in general was the second largest employment category for documented migrant workers after manufacturing, accounting for 114,000 workers from a total of 417,00, according to an International Labour Organisation study.[127] The proportion of legal domestic workers accounted for by migrants doubled to 50 per cent in the six years to 1999.[128] But the report noted that living in was the best way to avoid controls and that overseas workers are more likely to live in, often as a prelude to shifting to hourly paid employment in the same or another sector.[129] The scale of informal employment is illustrated by 300,000 households declaring in 2002 that they were employing migrant workers without residence rights.[130] The 1990s saw a major rise in the use of fixed-term contracts. Parallel to this, a trend emerged whereby a young worker from central Europe came to Italy on a three-month tourist visa, worked in a household and then returned home to be replaced by the next worker.[131] These two developments suggest a growing depersonalisation of the work. If that is the case, while the ILO report notes the work involves 'servile conditions which are highly restrictive of free time'[132] there might be less room for employers to use emotional blackmail as a tool of control of workers. On the other hand, it also suggests a more explicit commodification of the worker.

In Britain, the Kalayaan group works with those entering the country on domestic worker visas, some 17,000 of which were issued in 2005.[133] In 1998 horror stories of the abuse of such workers, brought into the country by expatriate diplomats and corporate executives and Britons returning from overseas postings, forced a change in the law so that they were recognised as workers (rather than members of the household), awarded some employment rights, and permitted to change employers (but not line of work). That gain – now under threat, as will be discussed later – was important but did not address the crucial problem of access to the newly recognised rights. Isolation, language problems and lack of freedom of movement or free time, means that those in the most abusive employment are the least likely to be able to assert or even know their entitlements.

In the year to March 2005, of the 322 migrant domestic workers registering with Kalayaan, 40 per cent were from India, 34 per cent from the Philippines and 10 per cent from Sri Lanka. More than 10 per cent were men.[134] Of the 387 who registered in the following year, no less than 23 per cent reported physical abuse and 70 per cent psychological abuse. Shockingly, more than 70 per cent said they did not receive enough food and 86 per cent worked more than 16 hours a day. More than half had no private room to sleep in and more than a quarter were locked in the house where they worked. A third had their passports illegally withheld by their employers.[135] Such conditions clearly meet the legal definition of forced labour, and they are suffered by workers who have entered the country with correct documentation and have defined rights.

Sexual harassment is not uncommon:

> She was not given money for food, and was not allowed to make a phone call. She worked from 7 a.m. to 11.30 p.m. with no breaks, and she was on call twenty-four hours a day. Often, after a party R catered to, the 'madam' would ask for her services at two or three o'clock in the morning. She was forced to wear a uniform, with no apron. If she wanted to go to church, she was asked to wear her uniform. And, for weeks at a time she would be left at the old house as a 'caretaker' with no access to the outside world and no money to make that contact happen. For weeks she was completely isolated inside the house she called a prison, held ransom by the fact that she still had not been paid.
>
> After five months, R received two months of pay when she left the old house and the 'madam'. She moved to London and found a job as a live-in domestic with a husband and his wife, who was a stay-at-home mother. It was during this period that she registered at Kalayaan. She was being sexually harassed by the husband, and she had no privacy – no lock on her door and he had no boundaries. She was on call twenty-four hours a day and was not paid on time or her full wages. Abusive words such as 'you are smelly', were common from the wife. R found herself skinny and with no appetite. The husband told her if she opened her mouth to tell about his sexual overtures, he would tell his wife she was doing something to the baby. She kept her mouth shut as long as she could bear it.[136]

While locking a worker in a house or assaulting her or holding her passport are unambiguous methods of forcing labour, subtler methods can achieve the same end. Kalayaan sees migrant domestic workers who have been told they will be pursued and beaten by the police if they escape. Some are told their immigration status is irregular and they will be deported if they prove difficult. In other instances the closeness to the employing household is manipulated.

Kate Roberts says that when Kalayaan contacts employers on behalf of workers who have left, it is frequent for them to be asked to tell the worker that the children of the house miss their nanny. Here the ambiguities of the relationship are exploited. To entice the worker back, the employer humanises the relationship, detaching it from the contract beween employer and worker and characterising it as a personal, non-monetary link between a sympathetic adult and affectionate children. It is the very fact that emotional links may well have been established that makes this a potent tool for re-establishing a highly exploitative employment. An instance of illegally low pay combined with emotional attachment that shades into blackmail is seen in this case study:

> L made the decision to accompany her employer back to his native London on account of her children, both of whom live with their own families outside Bombay, India. With their own young families to care for and no prospects for work, L's children and grandchildren now depend on her as the sole source of income. L has now been in London for four years as a full-time, live-in carer for an elderly disabled woman.
>
> When L arrived in London at age 47, she signed a private contract with her employer that stated she could not change employer and would work part-time for £200 per month as well as food, a private bedroom and bath. At the time, L did not know how to write or speak English. Very quickly, her employer developed trust in L and depended on her to be available at any time of time of day or night. She was kind, and L felt she could give the woman love and care.
>
> Because L did not know her rights, such as a minimum wage and the right to change employer, she lived with a constant fear that if she did anything wrong she might risk being fired. It was not until she came to Kalayaan and learned of her rights, and began taking English classes, that she recognised that her employer was grossly underpaying her.
>
> As she sees it, 'I do something for her, always. I expect her also to do something for me. Even though I don't know what's in her mind and don't trust her now.'

Exploited

So L has asked for raises, and she has received them. But her employer (who now pays her £500 per month) says she cannot pay L any more. L recognises the woman's hardship and feels sorry for her. She has developed a sense of loyalty to her employer, who tells her she cannot live without L. Her job extends beyond physical labour; she gives her emotions and her strength. 'Any troubles come and she (my employer) knows I will clear them up nicely.'

L gets her strength from church and from her friends. Even so, she is isolated and is not allowed to have friends stay over, for example. And she only has one day off per week. She says that even with all the assistance, 'we still don't have freedom'.[137]

Since 1998 those workers able to discover their legal rights have had a chance to improve their lot by changing employer. However, the obstacles are considerable. Live-in workers fleeing an abusive employer may well do so with no money and few possessions. They have no recourse to state housing benefit so many hostels will turn them away. Even if they have a contract its terms may well not be enforceable as it will not be valid if the employer has not been paying tax and national insurance, so back pay will be difficult to obtain. On top of that, the worker may well have to run the gamut of police and immigration service suspicion in trying to get her passport returned from the former employer.

A similar situation to that in Britain exists in the USA where the Break the Chain campaign supports migrant domestic workers brought in on special visas to accompany diplomats and officials of international agencies. Several thousand such visas are issued each year. The campaign cites the case of an employer who tried to get rid of a worker by having her committed to a mental hospital, and that of a worker who was beaten and housed in a basement for twenty years. It reports:

An American Ivy League professor, who specialises in women's issues and economic development, brought her Nepalese domestic worker to the US from India on a B-1 visa and paid her what she called 'her Indian salary' which totalled $45 a month. The domestic worker usually worked from 8:00 am to 9:30 pm, seven days a week, with no time off.[138]

Child slavery in suburbia

If the exploitation of documented adult migrant domestic workers is largely hidden from view by the nature of their work, their status does at least have legal recognition and – at the time of writing at any rate – the right to leave their employer. The same cannot be said of undocumented workers. The most vulnerable of these are trafficked child domestic workers. Their existence has been highlighted by a small non-governmental organisation called Africans Unite Against Child Abuse (Afruca). It was formed in 2001 after the exposure of a trade in young West African women through London and into the sex industry in Italy. By 2002 Afruca was working to combat the use of trafficked children within the African community in Britain as domestic workers.

The scale of the phenomenon is unknown. A multi-agency task force looked at unaccompanied children coming through Heathrow airport over a period of three months and concluded that it had 'failed to identify any significant levels of trafficking or exploitation'[139] but conceded that its work had a number of limitations, including not having looked at children coming in on EU passports and only looking at one point of entry. Even so, it was unable to account for 14 minors, mostly African girls, of 551 it had risk-assessed, and acknowledged reasons to be concerned about their welfare.

Yet Million Joseph, national advocacy officer at Afruca, believes there are thousands of African – mostly West African – children in servitude in Britain.[140] And he says the trend is upwards. He estimates he hears of an average of around fifteen instances each month. An operation such as Paladin fails to pick up cases for several reasons: the number of officers involved is too small to cope with the passengers coming off a large flight, let alone several simultaneous landings; the officers are not able to spot telltale signs, such as an adult and a child speaking different languages; and the right to question passengers with EU passports is very restrictive. More fundamentally, Paladin was looking at unaccompanied minors where Afruca maintains that most children are brought in by an adult and with the consent of their parents. As with most cases of trafficking, the victim is brought in legally, having agreed to make the journey. It is only on arrival that the true situation becomes apparent. And for a 12-year-old child who may never have been away from her family and may have no clear expectations of life outside, the situation may not be clear at all even then. With so little life experience the child may not question her fate.

In the typical scenario a distant relative approaches a poor family and offers to take a child – in most cases a girl of 11 or 12 – to a 'better life' in Britain where she will be schooled and be able to send home enough money to make a real difference to the family. The family agrees but once the child has gone contact is broken and the family, likely illiterate and without access to communications, loses touch. The process is presented in West African communities as a deformed version of a tradition whereby a better-off branch of a family would take in a child from a poorer branch. Indeed, the family to which the child is sent may well justify the process by saying the child is better off than she would be at home. Rightly or wrongly, the trafficking of children within West Africa for agricultural labour and quarrying has also been presented as a deformation of this tradition.

The child is used for domestic labour but her presence may also be used for the purpose of benefit fraud. Sexual exploitation is clearly a risk for young women. One is quoted as saying, 'In the day I am a house worker, in the night I am a housewife.' Control may be exerted physically, or by shame or fear of stigma if she returns home, or through concern about failing her family.

By the age of 16 or 18 the child is almost an adult and is generally disposed of or runs away, according to Million Joseph. The woman of the house may feel threatened by the presence of a young woman, and benefit fraud ceases to be a possibility. Once on the street there is no provision for these young people. In the eyes of the law they are simply illegal immigrants. Generally they find it hard to realise or admit they have been trafficked. On the streets they are clearly vulnerable to further abuse. The potential to help these young people would be significantly raised if the British government agreed to sign the European Convention Against Trafficking because that would give legal status to the victims.

On the continuum of gross exploitation, the live-in migrant domestic worker is one of the most vulnerable categories. Although possibly living in a city, she is even more isolated at work than a farm labourer. At the same time, the link between workplace and accommodation is even more marked than it is for workers housed by labour providers in agriculture. The potential for control and abuse by the employer covers twenty-four hours a day, sometimes every day. By and large these domestic workers come to the host country on a visa, knowing the job they will do and perhaps having an appreciation of the risks. The same is not true of children trafficked for domestic labour. However it may be dressed up by employers, and regardless of the child's material standard of living, this practice contravenes all of the most fundamental legal and moral precepts. It is forced child labour. It is people-trafficking. It is the stripping away of the victim's social, cultural and familial identity. It is slavery.

The Sex Industry

The sex industry is popularly associated with the worst forms of exploitation of migrant workers – trafficking and enslavement. Kevin Bales's landmark book *Disposable People*[141] details the tragedy of Siri, a Thai teenager trafficked into prostitution in Kuala Lumpur, while a British tabloid, with a hint of prurience, reports 'A heavily pregnant teenager who was systematically raped, beaten and imprisoned after being trafficked to Britain was dumped on a city's streets.'[142]

Prostitution is just part of an amorphous sex industry of blurred edges, grey areas, dubious legalities. The business probably takes in lap dancing and telephone sex lines, but does the stag-night strippergram count? When is entertainment exploitation? When is the 'saucy' sordid? Who controls the relationship between prostitute and punter and who profits? At one pole of the sex work–prostitution debate it is held that engaging in sex for money is no different from any other form of labour and, indeed, that it can provide the worker with more autonomy than most. At the other pole is the view that women offering sex for money are being exploited by patriarchy and capital and that the industry is inherently demeaning of women. This debate is not directly addressed here and the terms 'sex work' and 'prostitution' are used as neutrally as possible, the first standing for all employment within the wider sex industry and the second for renting out one's body for sex.

In Norway, research is being carried out on marriages involving Norwegian men and women from Thailand, Russia and the Philippines. These arrangements sometimes present as a mixture of sex work, domestic labour and care work by the woman, on occasion in conditions that were they outside of marriage would be classified as forced labour through trafficking inasmuch as the woman is trapped and feels she has been duped. Some men replace their wives before the latter gain Norwegian citizenship rights, thus treating the women as disposable migrant workers. Significantly, early work suggests that a sizeable proportion of these relationships when they break down result in the woman turning to prostitution.[143]

One estimate is that 80,000 people are involved in sex work in Britain.[144] And while senior policemen are on record claiming that most prostitutes are forced into the role by drug dependence and violence, others would point to those who choose to be part-time or short-term prostitutes because they can tailor the hours around their children's school time or their own college schedule or because they need to save money for a one-off purchase.

Two stereotypes of prostitution are common. The first is of the drug-dependent woman seeking out punters on the streets of King's Cross in London, under threat of violence from client and pimp and dealer. A community worker in Newport, South Wales, says that not a single prostitute in the city chooses to do the work; all are forced to do so by circumstances such as drug dependence, having dependants to support or coercive partners.[145] The second is the rosier image of the 'fun-loving' 'girl' 'up West':

> Wendy loves Soho and has worked there for twenty years. She is what's known as a prostitute's maid – a receptionist who works alongside a prostitute in a flat, greeting the customers, keeping records and looking after the girl. 'Most of the girls call me mum,' she says. 'Prostitutes have been around for years and men have always used them and they always will. It's not going to change.' 'We're off street, we're not hurting anybody,' she says, 'the majority of the girls they're here because they want to be.'[146]

Before looking at the extreme exploitation of migrant labour in the sex industry and at the contested approaches to tackling it on the part of officialdom, it is worth citing a more nuanced and perhaps more representative view of the transnational sex worker. Laura María Agustín wrote:

> Migrant workers in the European sex industry come from every conceivable background in terms of class, ethnicity, nationality and age, and they aren't just women but men and transgenders as well. They arrive in Europe via countless routes, alone, with friends, in couples or in accompanied groups. Some of them arrive with money to spend while others arrive indebted. They may be using their own real documents and a tourist visa, or falsified papers and a real work permit or any combination of true and false 'papers'....
>
> Many migrants doing sexual jobs do not describe themselves as 'forced' or as having no other options in life. They may well have fewer options, or fewer agreeable options, than some other people, but they have them....
>
> It is typical for them not to settle in one place to live. Very often they continue migrating ... The sex worker you encounter today in Madrid, you may find tomorrow in Paris, next month in Amsterdam and a year later back in Spain.[147]

As with other sectors of the economy the trends and flows of migrant workers shift according to many and complex factors. Some, like economic depression or civil conflict, push the worker to leave home, and others, such as ease of entry, potential earnings, community networks, pull her to one location rather than another. In London, and probably in Britain as a whole, even before the 2004 enlargement of the European Union, there appears to have been a sharp change in the national profile of sex workers. A study of those registering at a central London clinic in 1985–1992 found almost 75 per cent of sex workers to have been born in Britain, but by 1996–2002 that had fallen to under 37 per cent, so that almost two-thirds were migrants.[148] In the Norwegian capital, Oslo, a survey found a third of prostitutes at any one time to be short-term visitors, but due to the turnover of short-term workers a majority over a twelve-month period would be migrants.[149]

The flesh trade

If caution is needed to avoid succumbing to stereotypes of migrant (or domestic) sex workers, it is also needed when considering trafficking. In Europe attention has focused on trafficking of women and children and on the sex and (often related) domestic labour industries. But there are studies that argue that men required for a variety of jobs comprise the largest category of victims. In one, cited by the International Labour Organisation, 80 per cent of people trafficked into Ukraine and over 90 per cent trafficked into Poland were men.[150] The problem is that research into trafficking, by the nature of the phenomenon, tends to be small-scale, to use data sources that do not match, and to be focused on particular groups. So, the UN Office on Drugs and Crime is careful to explain that its analysis of global patterns of trafficking can only reflect what is reported, and that what is monitored varies widely from country to country, meaning that 'the data collected and presented ... should be interpreted with the utmost caution'.[151] The regular US government report is less cautious, stating: 'Each year, an estimated 600,000–800,000 men, women, and children are trafficked across international borders ... and the trade is growing ... The US government estimates that over half of all victims trafficked internationally are trafficked for sexual exploitation'.[152] Of the total, 70 per cent are female and 50 per cent are children, with most being used in the sex industry.[153]

Patterns of trade in people can be mapped just like trade in commodities, with arrows indicating the direction of the flow from region to region. Like commodities, the predominant flow of people tends to be from poorer to richer countries, developing to developed. But beneath that general truth there are more complex patterns. Some countries only export or import, some are points of transit, some a combination of all three.

Europe comprises two major subregions, according to the UN.[154] Western Europe is primarily a destination while central and south-eastern Europe is an origin, a transit area and, to a lesser extent, a destination. Most sources indicate adult women as victims with sexual exploitation the primary motivation. Albania, Bulgaria, Lithuania and Romania are most frequently cited as origin countries, but another six central and south-eastern European countries also rank high. The primary destination countries are Germany, Italy, the Netherlands, Greece, Britain, Belgium, Austria, France and Spain. At the same time, Bosnia, the Czech Republic, Kosovo and Poland are destination countries for people trafficked from the former Soviet Union. The UN reports several major origins for people trafficked into Western Europe: primarily central and south-eastern Europe but also countries of the former Soviet Union, Nigeria, Colombia and the Dominican Republic. A Spanish agency policing migration stated that of 3,053 undocumented foreigners it had identified as involved in prostitution over a two-year period, 1,106 were Romanian, while arrests of Nigerian, Brazilian and Russian 'ringleaders' indicated the origins of many of the other workers.[155]

Of course, the involvement of the rich world in the trafficking of women, minors and some men for sexual exploitation spreads far afield, most notoriously in the form of sex tourism in Southeast Asia where the industry sustains and expands intra-country and cross-border trafficking. Indeed, some have argued that the sex industry has become so important in Thailand that its constant need for fresh, frequently forced labour has shaped state planning.[156]

In Britain the issue of trafficking achieved a high profile by the media exposure given to Operation Pentameter, a project with a three-month operational phase involving fifty-five local police forces. As will be seen, Pentameter faced some fundamental criticism of its motivation, approach and claimed successes.

Nonetheless, it offered some insight into the worst excesses of exploitation within the sex industry. The officer in charge of the operation, Deputy Chief Constable Grahame Maxwell, said in an interview for this book[157] that he believed there are 2,000–3,000 women trafficked for sex working in Britain at any one time. What is a mystery is what happens to them when they are deemed no longer useful by their pimps. Some may be able to return to their country of origin while others continue to live in Britain where, if their status is irregular, their options for earning a living are limited to illegal employment and they will be ineligible for medical care or state benefits.

The regions of origin are central Europe (both EU and non-EU states), parts of Asia, particularly China, Thailand and Malaysia, and West Africa. A few Latin American women have been identified and there was one case that appeared to involve a British woman trafficked within the country. The accession of central European states to the EU has increased the flow of women from those countries into Britain because they can enter without visas. There is concern in officialdom that the 2012 London Olympics will bring an increase in trafficking into Britain for sex, just as there was concern over trafficking for prostitution into Germany, where some 40,000 migrant prostitutes were expected to arrive during the World Cup.[158]

DCC Maxwell said some trafficked women were working up to sixteen hours a day, having unprotected sex at a charge of up to £70 an hour. That would mean a pimp running a single prostitute could have takings of over £1,000 a day with the most significant daily expense being premises. The initial outlay for a woman trafficked into Britain, according to Pentameter, would vary from £8,000 paid for a Lithuanian virgin to £500 for a woman in her late thirties whose useful working life was coming to an end. The youngest victim identified by Pentameter was 14 years old.

Traffickers will place women in different cities or countries according to ethnic origin and the racial preferences of local punters. Frequently women are rotated between towns to provide a 'fresh' supply. While a high proportion of the activity of Pentameter was in metropolitan areas including London, Birmingham and Glasgow, there were also raids in rural areas.

Three types of trafficker have been identified as operating into Britain and these are probably common to western Europe as a whole. There are full supply-chain networks trafficking women from China and Albania where the victim is identified, lured, transported and sold or delivered by a single gang. There are separate gangs operating as loose networks passing women from country to country, and there are sole traders, particularly in Africa, who will bring in an individual woman, perhaps with a loose kinship to the trafficker, sometimes speculatively to sell her on.

All of the women identified as victims by Pentameter had entered Britain through legal channels although perhaps on false documents. This is characteristic of trafficking into a state with relatively well policed borders and entry points. It is not easy to bring an unwilling person through immigration control, so victims are lured by promises of jobs and money and security and only discover they have been enslaved when it is too late. Generally, traffickers do not act as pimps or run brothels but are specialists in their own right. The process of luring and accompanying victims is very different from transporting drugs or weapons and gangs involved in the one enterprise are not likely to be directly involved in the other, although proceeds from one illegal activity may be invested in another.

A study of migrant prostitution and trafficking in Oslo defined four strategies for controlling the women it had identified as victims of trafficking. These ranged from direct physical violence and incarceration to control through manipulation, then to an acceptance by the woman that she has no choice and her life is out of her control, and lastly to development of 'romantic feelings towards [her] oppressors'.[159] But things may well not be clear-cut. Control may be exerted through a combination of close surveillance – trafficked prostitutes are generally confined rather than working on the streets – physical intimidation, threats against families, the insecurity of having no papers (these will have been held by the trafficker), shame and, in the case of the young or uneducated, simply having no idea where they are.

The process is exemplified by a West African teenager who was dumped in Sheffield. Nine months previously, an orphan, she had been begging in a village in Nigeria. A 'friend of the family' offered to provide work and took her to a town, where she remained in lodgings for a week while papers were obtained for her. She was then taken by train to a port and a put on a ship, which took two weeks to reach its destination somewhere in southern Europe. She calculated that it then took three six-hour train journeys to get her to King's Cross in London, where she was forced to work as a prostitute in a flat with other women who spoke languages she did not understand. She was beaten when she became pregnant and forced to do domestic labour in the flat before being driven to Sheffield and abandoned.

In another case, a 15-year-old Lithuanian school student was enticed to Britain by two young women, also in their teens, on the promise of a job selling ice cream. She was flown from Riga to Heathrow on a low-cost airline and accompanied through immigration control, whereupon she had her passport taken away. She was then sold, according to prosecution evidence, for £4,000, taken to Birmingham, raped and forced to work as a prostitute. She was soon sold on for £3,000. She managed to escape but with nowhere to go was recaptured and sold on, with her market price deteriorating each time. She eventually escaped with the help of some English women who aided her when she was taken to a nightclub. Several men were later jailed for between four and eighteen years.

Amnesty International cites the case of an older woman:

> Maria, a Ukrainian woman, left her country to work in Italy to raise money for her daughter's education. When her visa ran out she met a man in Italy who said that he could arrange work for her in the UK. She entered the UK with him, but once she arrived here she was beaten, raped and forced into prostitution. She was sold three times while in the UK and was made to work in various parts of London.[160]

Victim, but whose victim?

Each of the three cases above is an unambiguous example of enslavement, but often there are divergent narratives, varying interpretations of circumstances. In its operational phase, Pentameter was said to have freed 84 trafficked women, detained 100 non-trafficked, undocumented sex workers, and made some 200 arrests in the course of 550 raids. The English Collective of Prostitutes (ECP) was a major critic of Pentameter, dismissing estimates of the number of women trafficked into Britain as false extrapolations from raids that anyway often wrongly identified women as trafficked when they were simply undocumented. Certainly, if the estimate cited earlier of 80,000 people working in the wider sex industry in Britain and DCC Maxwell's estimate of 2,000–3,000 trafficked women working as prostitutes at any one time are both anywhere close to correct (and there have been higher government estimates for the latter category), then the proportion of foreign prostitutes in the country who are enslaved would be so high as to blow away the more nuanced view of migrant sex workers quoted earlier.

The ECP has long defended and represented sex workers. It certainly does not deny that some women are trafficked and otherwise coerced into prostitution. Indeed it provides support for them. It asserts that women who work on the street in particular face considerable dangers, while undocumented women confront increasing discrimination. But it points out that many migrant women working in London as prostitutes have decided to do so – not from circumstances of their choosing, perhaps – as a short-term measure in order to save money to build a house, start a small business or provide a lump sum for a family back home.[161] This echoes the view of Laura María Agustín that migrant sex workers are often people with options.

This view is shared by the medical researchers who noted the growing number of migrant sex workers in London. They wrote: 'Many of the women who migrate and work in the sex industry today are well educated and motivated to improve their life chances. They rarely use drugs and consider prostitution a transitory way of acquiring education and language skills.'[162]

For the ECP, Pentameter is the latest manifestation of a policy of immigration control and policing of prostitutes rather than rescuing and caring for victims of trafficking. Raids on well-run premises have simply been trawls for undocumented women who have then been deported, says the ECP. This has amounted to persecution of uncoerced sex workers operating in the relative safety of premises, while reported crimes of violence against women, including prostitutes, are scarcely investigated, it said in a letter to the Home Office.

At the same time, the ECP questions the successes claimed for Pentameter and the state's treatment of the women 'rescued' in raids. By way of example it points to a much publicised raid of a massage parlour in Birmingham when nineteen women were taken into custody and proclaimed to be victims of trafficking.

The women denied this. No charges of trafficking were brought against anyone caught up in the raid, but six of the women were sent to a detention centre to await deportation. Some of these women, according to the ECP, said they were told that the only way to avoid deportation was to say they had been trafficked. In conversation, ECP campaigners talked of a raid in Manchester that resulted in the maid being deported while the prostitutes fled, presumably to work on the streets. Fear of deportation discourages women who have been trafficked or otherwise abused from coming forward. While it may be able to call on voluntary agency-run facilities, the state itself provides just one hostel for trafficked women, access to which is limited by a set of conditions, including a bar on self-referral.

For the ECP, Pentameter has simply continued policies pursued in previous years under different names. Back in 2001, it protested against raids on fifty flats in Soho in Central London. The raids were on the pretext of protecting women from pimps and traffickers. In fact they were independent prostitutes, many of whom happened also to be undocumented migrants, and some of whom were summarily deported.

The stance of the ECP chimes with the analysis of others. Back in 2000, Australian academic and rights campaigner Penelope Saunders wrote that 'substantial evidence exists to indicate that anti-trafficking initiatives are more concerned with eliminating prostitution and stemming migration than in protecting human rights'.[163] It also bears striking similarity to the comments of a Chinese activist who argues that the lives of undocumented migrants in his community are being made worse and worse by a government that boldly categorises people as either victims or villains while ignoring the realities of their lives.

The conditions in which migrant sex workers operate have been made more difficult by government policies of recent years, while at the same time driving more women towards prostitution through the (now withdrawn) voucher system imposed on asylum, seekers and new limits on their rights to work, and the withdrawal of student grants. Many hospitals and surgeries now ask to see passports before treating people who appear to be foreign. Shockingly, even women's refuges turn away undocumented women because they cannot claim state benefits and pay them to the refuge, thus removing a final sanctuary to those escaping enforced sex work. This latter problem is also confronted by domestic workers trying to escape abusive employers.

Confused moral and political attitudes towards sex work are compounded by the indistinct categories, such as the foreign brides in Norway. Combined with lack of uncontested information about the industry this leads to a situation where the (mostly) women migrants involved are too often unhelpfully lumped into a pile labelled victim or a pile labelled shameless harlot. What is required is a policy that distinguishes between those who are forced into prostitution through trafficking or other coercive means, and those who have chosen to work as prostitutes because it suits them better than alternative employment options. For the former group, robust rescue operations must be combined with proper provision of support to enable them to regain control over their lives. For the latter, what is needed is a proper defence of their rights to work without intimidation or exploitation by pimps, punters or policemen.

Industry by industry, this chapter has logged the methods by which migrant labour is super-exploited: the opt-outs written into contracts, the deductions from wages, the manipulation of hours, the deceit and trickery, and, sometimes, the brutality and enslavement. It has also shown the importance of migrant labour to vital parts of the economies in which we live and work. Migrant labour is not an incidental fraction of the workforce; it is important to the operation of our food, construction, hospitality, cleaning and other industries. More than that – and this is a crucial point – while it is used to fill gaps in the indigenous workforce, it does not simply fill a void left by locals or satisfy demand created by demographic change. Rather, it fills the gaps under wages and conditions worse than those of local co-workers. The argument that very many migrants do receive the same wages and work the same hours as their local counterparts misses the point that the significant numbers who are discriminated against boost the productivity of the enterprise. Also, as will be seen later, the terms under which migrants even from EU accession states are allowed into the UK and other earlier EU member states give their employment a precariousness and insecurity that benefits the employer.

So, migrant labour, by boosting productivity and improving margins, allows the tender for a building contract to be lower or the demands of the supermarket buyer to be met, or the hotel chain to compensate for low productivity, or the Indian restaurant to meet the challenge of longer pub opening hours. There probably are poorly managed companies that compensate for inefficiencies elsewhere by attacking wages and conditions, and there probably are rogue employers who will line their own pockets in any way they can, but to think that addressing the abuse of migrant labour is a matter of penalising a few 'bad apples' is to miss the point of this chapter. The use of migrant labour is systemic to sectors we have looked at, and its exploitation over and above the exploitation of local workers is a means of addressing competitive pressures. In some cases those pressures may appear to be entirely local, but others are clearly global and that is why we see migrant labour employed in the same industries and abused in the same ways across much of the global North. The next chapter addresses the issue of the broader impact of migrant labour on the economies of host countries.

3

Impacts

The impact of migration on the economy and on social provision is the key area of contest between those who support more or less unfettered movement of labour and those who want to pull up the drawbridge. This chapter discusses the complexities of defining the impact of recent migration on the economy, particularly employment and wage levels. It then turns to the impact of migrant influx on social provision, often an issue of concern for host communities. There will be brief mention of the other side of the coin – the impact of labour emigration on the countries from which migrants arrive. Although Britain is the focus, it stands for western European countries as a whole (and, indeed, the USA), where, as the OECD has remarked, migrants are concentrated in the same group of industries and where the same influences of a recent extension of subcontracting and fictitious self-employment are at play.[1]

The perils and profits of migrant labour for host countries are disputed between those wanting the drawbridge to be pulled up, the portcullis lowered and the great unwashed kept beyond the castle walls, and those more welcoming of newcomers. Plainly, the dispute is intertwined with that over immigrants – those who come into the country with the intention of settling or who decide to settle once they have arrived. In part this is because, as noted before, the categories are not hard and fast. Decisions are changed, circumstances alter, appearances prove deceptive, so some who intended to stay do not and some who thought their sojourn would be temporary end up staying. The tenfold difference in the estimates of the proportion of post-accession Polish workers who intend to stay in Britain, referred to elsewhere, illustrates the point. In France and Belgium, the first wave of Moroccan migrant workers is becoming more and more settled, with remittance income becoming more precarious for their country of origin. In the USA it appears the toughening of border controls with Mexico fails to keep undocumented workers out but succeeds in keeping in many who would prefer to work seasonally in both countries, thus turning would-be migrants into immigrants.

The problems and challenges faced by many migrant workers frequently persist in immigrant communities. These include lack of opportunity in the workplace, low wages, poor housing, language difficulties. But the temporary nature of migrant labour as a category does mark it out as different. Unaccompanied workers intending to stay somewhere for two or three years before returning home do not pose the long-term questions of social inclusion, of second generations unable to break out of low-income employment, of educational underachievement that accompany discussion of immigration. Because they are constantly replaced, migrant workers' role in the economy and the conditions of their employment may be less amenable to change or, if not change, challenge than those of immigrant communities building long-term futures for succeeding generations. Their ability or determination to organise may be lessened by the knowledge that the conditions they put up with will not be long endured – by them as individuals, at any rate.

For trade unions, organising a constantly changing workforce is an uphill struggle.

Migrant labour and the economy

Analysis by conventional economists indicates that the influx of accession-state migrant labour into the fifteen established members of the EU has been positive. A report for the European Commission said that they 'positively contribute in each member state to overall labour market performance, to sustained economic growth and to the state of public finances'.[2]

In Britain, economists have found recent migrant entry to be increasing the productive potential of the economy, boosting actual GDP growth, holding back inflation and, potentially, interest rates. The ITEM Club of economists calculated that between 1997 and 2005 net inward migration added 0.4 per cent a year to potential growth in Britain because it increased the availability of a key factor of production – labour. (The 'lump of labour' argument that held that there is only so much work available in an economy and that extra workers would only be excess was long ago declared a fallacy.) Without that migration, the potential growth rate would have been just 0.1 per cent. A consequence of the ITEM Club's calculation is that there is more spare capacity in the economy than has been recognised. That reduces inflationary pressure and should militate against higher interest rates.[3] Another study concluded that

> The overall impact of immigration[4] on GDP growth is substantial. Taking 2004 and 2005 together, the economy grew by 5.3 per cent. Of this, 0.9 percentage points can be attributed to the direct effect of immigration after allowing for some unemployment effect.[5]

These findings in the UK echo those cited earlier for Spain where economic growth would have tipped into recession over the past decade were it not for inward migration.

Discussion of the fiscal impact of population inflow ranges from the assertions of the racist right that foreigners come to Britain to sponge off the benefit system and health service through to economists' aggregation of available data. In fact, most migrant workers have only very limited access to state benefits. Indeed, one of the objectives of the Worker's Registration Scheme was to preclude short-term accession-state migrants from access to public housing or to housing benefits. Only a tiny proportion of their claims for more general benefits are approved.[6] Undocumented workers, of course, neither draw from the social security system nor contribute to it. Legalisation of their status and drawing them into the tax system could raise a net £1 billion a year for the Treasury.[7] Discussion of the fiscal balance sheet has tended to lump immigrants and migrants together. From the work that does distinguish the two, it seems that immigrants, like migrants, are net contributors rather than beneficiaries.[8]

Employment and wage levels

Perhaps the staunchest advocate of migrant labour has been the employers' lobby. At conferences and in the press it has extolled the economic gains to be had and the virtues of migrant workers. A major reason cited by the 27 per cent of employers found in one survey to be intending to recruit from abroad was shortage of experience and skills in the indigenous workforce, with around one-fifth citing higher levels of 'commitment' among migrant workers.[9] A study of the use of temporary workers in the agriculture and food industry found that

> Foreign nationals working in the sector were relied on to apply the levels of effort now required to achieve the minimum wage through piece work over days, weeks and months of work. Foreign nationals were sought who were considered more likely to be compliant, reliable and flexible than UK nationals.[10]

Indeed, some employers expressed concern that EU accession-state workers would lose their 'hunger' for work after a while. In France, there is the same motivation for taking on Moroccan workers on short-term contracts to work in agriculture. In theory, contracts are only approved by the authorities if there is no available indigenous labour, but

> In fact, these mechanisms are skipped, and the big agricultural enterprises prefer a precarious and docile workforce, coming from abroad for several months to employees living in France and well able to defend themselves against the injustices to which they are victim.[11]

And there's the rub. While the 'lump of labour' notion may be fallacious at the macroeconomic level, of course that does not mean that all available labour will be employed or that employers do not seek to reduce costs by taking on the cheapest labour. So, as one of the economic analyses quoted above recognises, the GDP growth resulting from inward labour migration 'does not imply an increase in the welfare of the indigenous population, except in so far as the fiscal system means that immigrants are net lifetime contributors to the budget'.[12] In the short term at any rate, it is 'likely that owners of capital gain from immigration and people who supply labour in direct competition with immigrants lose out'.[13] Then the ITEM Club report noted, as a benefit of migrant labour, that 'the downward pressure new workers have exerted on real wages has helped to prevent wages and prices from responding to rising energy and commodity prices.'[14]

For indigenous populations, perhaps the key concern is whether migrant labour actually substitutes for local labour. In other words, do employers replace local workers with cheaper migrants? At the aggregate level of the EU, the Commission's assessment is that this has not been the case with accession-state workers at any rate. It found that the influx of accession-state workers 'may have positive effects on labour markets by relieving labour shortages in certain areas. New jobs can be created, for example in the construction and in the domestic and catering services sectors, that would risk not being filled otherwise in some countries.'[15] Not only that, the Commission also found the sectoral composition of the national workforce pretty much unchanged between 2003 and 2005, so there was no evidence of migrants crowding local workers out of particular jobs.[16]

Prior to the 'shock' of the high numbers of accession-state workers entering Britain, it appeared that the net rise in the number of migrant workers in the 1990s was being absorbed into the labour market.[17] But when in the summer of 2006 unemployment figures rose relatively sharply, the press laid those numbers alongside the migrant inflow numbers and concluded there was a causal relationship. This view has found some backing. Riley and Weale's model suggested unemployment had risen by 0.2–0.3 percentage points due to the arrival of accession-state workers. A year earlier the Chartered Institute of Personnel and Development noted the 'apparent paradox' of rising employment numbers and rising claims for unemployment benefit and said this was likely caused by 'some sudden event which changed employer recruitment'.[18] That event, it said, was probably the influx of accession-state workers.

Within an overall context of filling vacancies and doing so inexpensively, the precise reasons for turning to migrant labour vary from sector to sector and from segment to segment within sectors. The argument of ethnic cuisine restaurants that they could not survive without migrant labour is founded not just on comparative labour costs but also on the need to have an ethnically based workforce, while for agriculture and food processing it is much more clearly a matter of the relative costs of pools of undifferentiated labour. In construction, unskilled migrant labour is used because it is cheap, but skilled workers may be taken on because the indigenous workforce has not been trained. Some businesses facing competition from abroad may argue that they would have to shut up shop if they could not reduce the wage bill. But this argument cannot be used by, say, contract cleaners because the installations they service are fixed. For them, the competition is local and if they did not have recourse to cheap documented and cheaper undocumented migrant labour it seems likely wage rates would have to rise to attract indigenous labour that spurns the work at current wage levels.

Documented migrant workers are entitled to the same minimum wage as indigenous workers, and when the two work alongside each other it may appear that they do earn the same. But this is where it is important to remember the many examples of exploitation of migrant workers recorded in the preceding chapter. These practices make migrant labour an integral factor in the economics of sectors in which they work. The 'hunger' for work, the 'reliability' and 'flexibility' of migrant labour are employers' terms for long hours, lack of overtime bonuses, unpaid duties, zero hour contracts, Working Time Directive opt-outs, and disposability of migrant labour. In industries like agriculture and contract cleaning, where competition means that control of margins is crucial, driving down the unit cost of labour is key to employers.

Similarly, when employers cite greater experience or possession of relevant skills as reasons for seeking migrant workers, they are only stating in other terms their failure to keep and train local hires. This is particularly true in the construction industry, where, as we have seen, the structure of the sector creates and worsens shortages of skilled labour. It is increasingly evident in the oil industry. The burden of the training costs is shifted on to the labour-exporting country, as is the loss of experience. All of these factors add to the productivity of a migrant labourer relative to indigenous labour. There is evidence that the majority of employers will not recruit from the core jobless and often look to migrants from outside the UK, with consequent implications for the ability to meet targets relating to reducing joblessness amongst 'hard-to-help' groups and raising skill levels and promoting workforce development amongst those with poor skills.[19]

Anecdotally, comments such as 'I'd rather take on a Kurd than a young English bloke who'll turn up late and is probably on drugs'[20] are standard among those who hire and fire staff. The conviction that the core unemployed are feckless and workshy is just as questionable as its precursor, the Tudor notion of the undeserving poor. Where migrant labour fills gaps in low-skilled employment it is generally because the work is so unpleasant that indigenous workers refuse it, preferring the floor provided by the benefits system if alternative work is not available. That is why meat-packing plants in areas of South Wales with relatively high levels of unemployment have resorted to migrant labour. But it is too much of a leap to argue that the migrant workers are doing jobs that would otherwise not be done. Locals who decline the work may well not be refusing the work per se but refusing it at the pay and conditions offered. It may be that without the reservoir of migrant labour, wages and conditions would be raised.

Undocumented migrant labour is a further pool from which employers may draw. The addition of undocumented workers to a labour force can directly dilute overall costs through tax and National Insurance avoidance and imposition of yet longer and more flexible hours, while undermining the position of documented workers. A community worker in Liverpool reports Czech Roma workers being paid for sixteen hours work a week so they could claim tax benefits due to low-paid workers while being obliged to work another twenty-four hours a week for no pay.[21]

Of course, it is not just undocumented migrant workers who fulfil this function but any employees who are working 'off the books'. In the 1970s it was common in Britain for small employers to pay very low wages to workers who were 'doing the double', signing on for unemployment benefit. Georges Tapinos, in an article looking at the way employers in OECD countries benefit from using undocumented labour, recalls that in France in the 1960s when the state periodically regularised undocumented migrants, employers would systematically hire workers before their status was regularised in order to keep wage levels down.[22]

In the USA, the same phenomenon can be seen but on a larger scale inasmuch as the proportion of undocumented workers in the population is higher. An economist from the Rand Corporation said

> They [migrants] compete with the least skilled Americans, and anyone who competes with undocumented immigrants is going to lose out and their wages are going to go down. I think a reasonable number for that is that those wages go down about 4 or 5 per cent.[23]

In 2003–04 Hispanic employment in the US rose by 1 million, driven by new arrivals, but at the same time the real weekly earnings of the Hispanic population fell by 2.2 per cent in the first year and another 2.6 per cent in 2004, the only major group of workers to suffer a two-year fall.[24]

The public perception of the economic impact of migration may be different from the statistical aggregate. A poll in Ireland found one in five people saying they knew someone who had been sacked or had their wages cut because of competition with migrant labour. Among low-skilled workers the rate went up to 36 per cent.[25] It is most unlikely that the poll reflected a statistical reality but it did demonstrate a public concern and, perhaps significantly, was taken in the wake of the high-profile Irish Ferries industrial dispute where the employers tried to bring in low-paid seafarers, and during public debate over future

access for Bulgarian and Romanian workers when their countries
joined the EU.

The growth of concentrated migrant communities has benefited
those businesses nimble enough to spot a growing market. Sales of
Polish beer have soared in western Europe. In Britain, SAB Miller
reported a 400 per cent rise in sales of its Tyskie brand, with major
growth in Ireland, the Netherlands, France and Germany as well.[26]
Supermarket chains Sainsbury, Asda and Tesco have all introduced
Polish foods into selected stores, while bars and restaurants catering for migrant communities have sprung up.[27]

Schools, health care and housing

In Britain, the speed of the influx of accession-state workers has
brought numerous reports of already stressed social provision
coming under further pressure despite the strict limitations on
migrant workers' access to benefits and the government campaign
against asylum seekers. The private housing rental market has been
particularly affected. Paragon, a mortgage lender specialising in
lending to landlords, saw its buy-to-let loans rise 82 per cent in
2006, attributing market strength to demand for rental properties
from migrant workers. In Edinburgh property agents said private-
sector rents had risen by 15–20 per cent in a year due to the arrival
of 20,000 central European workers.[28] The same phenomenon was
reported in parts of Wales and parts of England. While this may
be a boon for landlords, mortgage companies and subletting labour
providers, of course it drives up costs for local households. At the
same time, as the chapter on economic sectors illustrated, the
living conditions endured and the rents paid by migrant workers
can be grossly exploitative. So, to pick just one example, the local
authority in the small town of Rugby in the English Midlands
recorded a threefold increase in complaints about overcrowding

after a trebling of the number of migrant workers in the area, some of them living ten to a house.[29] In Slough, to the west of London, 1,000 houses were converted to multiple occupancy in the first two years after accession as the Polish community grew by 10,000.[30] While some live in inadequate and overcrowded accommodation, others end up homeless because of their lack of recourse to public funds. A survey by frontline agencies in London found 15 per cent of users of free nightshelters and other services to be accession-state nationals.[31] Add in people from the rest of the world who are using the shelters and the proportion of users who are migrants would be far higher.

Along with concerns about pressure on the housing stock, the local and national press in Britain has not been slow to highlight suggestions that migrant workers and their families might have a negative impact on education and health. 'The impact of migrant children has been blamed for a "significant" downturn in English standards at a city secondary school',[32] reported a paper in the East Anglia region where local agriculture depends on migrant workers. Media coverage of a Health Protection Agency report highlighted that 70 per cent of patients newly diagnosed with HIV, TB and malaria were born outside of Britain.[33] *Edinburgh Evening News* warned its readers about doctors 'having to close their doors because of the massive increase in Scotland's population' and warned of surgery queues extending yet further because doctors were spending more time with patients who needed a translator.[34] More rarely do media reports note that documented migrant workers pay taxes and National Insurance contributions despite their limited access to state benefits.

The perception that migrants are jeopardising social provision for locals becomes a political football. So, for example, in the town of Crewe, in the north of England, the local Conservative Party council leader called for severe restrictions on the future entry of Bulgarian and Romanian workers, saying local people 'feel that the [existing] migrant workers are putting pressure on the schools, health service, social services and housing provision'.[35] He said local people had not been consulted about 'overwhelming changes' to parts of the town with high migrant numbers, and spoke of 'apprehension and concern'. Veteran Labour Party politican Frank Field questioned the rate of entry of migrant workers on similar grounds, justifying his position on the grounds that 'dramatic' changes to the country were changing its character, hitting poorer areas, and risking exploitation of the issue by the far right.[36]

Although most migrants say they have been well received in Britain,[37] there is the danger that resentments, whether from real or imagined causes, will exacerbate the exploitation many of them face in their working lives. Examples of violence between migrant workers and the members of the indigenous community are not hard to find. What can be more difficult is judging when violence is visited on migrants because they are migrants and when origin is incidental. In 2004 there was a major incident in the town of Boston in Lincolnshire, which has a large Portuguese and Polish agricultural migrant community, where a riot during the Europe 2004 football competition targeted foreign nationals. A local councillor spoke of 'horrible racist chants', scaremongering about housing provision and jobs, and a soaring vote for the anti-EU UK Independence Party and the far-right British National Party.[38]

On the other side of England a group of Polish migrant workers were set upon in a remote house by a gang of around fifteen in what appeared to be a racist attack in October 2006, the same month in which three men were jailed elsewhere for nail-bombing flats where Portuguese and Polish workers lived. An attack by around twenty locals on Lithuanian workers in Royston, some forty miles north of London, was accompanied by racial abuse and yells for them to go home. In the north of Ireland, where sectarian Loyalist paramilitaries have long combined anti-republican views with racism, there has been a spate of attacks on migrant workers' lodgings.

An issue that is easy to overlook is the impact of the arrival of new groups of migrant workers on longer established groups. A report for the Rowntree Foundation notes non-accession-state migrants fearing that an influx of accession-state workers was making it more difficult for them to find and hold on to jobs.[39] Some further indications of accession-state workers edging out other migrants have been seen in the course of this book – the decline in the dominance of Portuguese workers in some agricultural areas, competition between longer-established Asian labour networks and new central European workers in the English Midlands. If this is a widespread phenomenon, it may be new to some sectors and it may be more dramatic than previously because the scale of influx is greater. Inasmuch as they have been observed, the tighter restrictions on the right of asylum seekers to work also seems likely to have allowed central European migrants to replace a swathe of predominantly developing country nationals.

The pillage of exporting countries

Reference has already been made to labour migration as a means by which the importing country reaps the benefits of the raising, education and training of workers by the exporting country. Generally, this is a transfer from developing or transitional economies to developed economies. In exchange for émigré sons and daughters, exporting countries received remittances through official channels of $180 billion in 2005, according to the World Bank.[40]

Migrant labourers are often more highly educated than their peers in the indigenous workforce even when they are used as undifferentiated, unskilled workers. An International Labour

Organisation report on Italy noted that from a large sample of workers in Lombardy, 'over 60 per cent had higher education, secondary or tertiary, but the great majority were employed in manual work, factory workers or services'.[41] In Greece, 'Most of the jobs migrants undertake are non-skilled, manual work well below their education and qualifications'.[42]

A regional study in England[43] noted that most migrant workers downgraded their employment significantly when they entered the country even though their skills corresponded to labour shortages in Britain. Over 15 per cent of migrant workers had management and professional skills but employment agencies were not interested in specific skills and so they were not utilised. Trade unions and employers alike frequently remark on the numbers of foreign teachers, nurses and engineers picking fruit or packing shelves in Britain.

Where migration removes a significant proportion of excess labour it may have a positive effect on wages in the exporting country. Employers will have to compete to attract workers rather than simply taking them off the dole queues at wages little above unemployment benefits. Some economists argue that the increase in the wage bill then stimulates greater efficiency on the part of employers as they try to recoup the extra costs. This greater efficiency then boosts the economy as a whole. However, if the labour that is lost through migration is skilled, a brake may be put on development because those skills are no longer available to employers and the capital invested in training has been lost.

The most controversial area of labour export is in the health services, where the training costs are high and the human costs of loss of provision higher. In Britain, one in three doctors, one in six dentists and one in ten nurses were trained overseas.[44] In the decade from 1997, over 80,000 overseas nurses were admitted to the UK register.[45] The pull from Britain and other rich countries is catastrophic for the health services of the exporting countries, particularly those grappling with the ravages of HIV/Aids. South Africa spent $1 billion educating health workers who then emigrated. That represents a third of all development aid for the period 1994–2000[46] and the country now imports health workers from other, poorer African nations. Between 30 and 50 per cent of health graduates leave for Britain or the USA each year. France imports health workers from francophone Africa, exploiting the linguistic and pedagogical legacy of direct colonial rule in the same way that Britain does.

Some two-thirds of Jamaican nurses emigrated in the 1990s, and in 1999 Ghana lost more nurses than it trained.[47] The Philippines lost 50,000 nurses to Europe, North America and the Middle East over a recent four-year period, while it trained just 20,000.[48] Transitional countries are also losing health professionals now. By some estimates, one doctor in ten has left Poland since 2004,[49] with 4,000 applying to come to Britain.[50]

Outrage over the sucking dry of developing-country health services pushed the British government into imposing controls over the import of doctors and nurses into the National Health Service. But no such controls exist in the private sector, where, to add insult to injury, trade unions and community groups report that health professionals are sometimes given much lower grade jobs than they were promised or are qualified to do, thus reducing their pay and further wasting their expertise.

The rich countries make much of their development aid to the medical services from which they poach but the savings they make on training personnel are substantial. It costs ten times as much to train a health professional in the global North as in the South.[51] So, notionally at any rate, for the €50 million that Ghana has spent since 1999 on training health workers who then emigrated,[52] the importing countries saved €500 million. Earlier we encountered calculations of the relative costs of raising a worker in a rich country and a developing country. The same point emerges in this more specific case of the health services. That is that while migration comprises millions of individual dilemmas, decisions and histories, those aggregate into a stripping by the global North of the labour and skills of the South. Inasmuch as the impetus to migrate is created by the trade rules and financial institutions dominated by the North, this constitutes systematic pillage. Not in the scale of human suffering but in terms of the provision of skills and labour power it is a modern-day equivalent of the slave trade.

The challenge

To sum up, in macroeconomic terms migrant labour boosts growth and the potential for growth. It increases production and consumption, including opening up new niche areas of consumption. It also tends to weaken upward pressure on inflation and interest rates. Migrants also contribute to government revenues through their taxes. Even if one accepts that GDP growth is a good thing in itself, the aggregate figures do not tell the story of what is happening in particular parts of the economy or to particular parts of society. There is no contradiction between a growing economy and growing inequalities within that economy or the enrichment of some at the expense of others. This is why migrant labour touches a raw nerve. If it squeezes local workers out of jobs or pushes down wages or leads to generally worse conditions of employment, it is clearly a cause for concern for the affected parts of the indigenous community. Similarly, if availability of housing or schooling or healthcare comes under pressure, there are bound to be resentments. Whether in jobs or social provision, contentions that the impact is limited to particular jobs in particular industries – be they food processing or prostitution – tied to specific localities, only short-run pending a restructuring of the economy, cut little ice among those affected.

With ageing populations in the rich countries of the world, there are jobs and potential jobs that would not be filled without an incoming labour force because the indigenous workforce growth rate is too slow. There are also current skills shortages in industries such as construction or the upstream oil industry or the health service, and migrants fill these without threatening local workers' jobs. However, they may do so because local workers do not have the training opportunities to take on these jobs. When migrants and local labour work together on the same job, the concern is that the former will depress wage rates and conditions. This is a danger. It is the reason for many employers' liking for migrant workers – higher productivity can be squeezed out of them. Then there are those 'dirty, dangerous and degrading' jobs that local workers avoid. Are these only avoided because for locals the marginal gain of the wage does not outweigh the disbenefits of doing the job? Without migrant workers would the wage go up or the employer shut down?

What is clear is that if the indigenous workforce lacks training opportunities for a skilled job or prefers to decline work at low wages for which migrants will take it, or sees wages and conditions eroded because migrant labour is used to cut the wage bill, the losers are the workers, local and migrant, and the winner is the employer. The employer is succeeding in pushing down his costs, the local workforce is squeezed and the migrant workforce is exploited. For the labour movement the challenge is to equalise conditions of employment for migrant and domestic labour by raising the former.

4

Government Response
and Responsibilities

The policies of governments have three strands in respect of migrant workers. There is the overarching determination of the desired number and attributes. This involves assessment of the demand from employers in terms of both raw labour power and skills. As indicated in the previous chapter, that calculation is not as simple as it may first seem because to be effective it needs to be predictive. A simple snapshot of job vacancies today is not enough. Policy needs to be informed by an understanding of the dynamics of future demand. That is complicated by the argument that changing the availability of labour itself changes the potential growth rate of an economy and the demand for labour – the antithesis of the 'lump of labour' fallacy. Other factors must be taken into account too, including the rights accorded to some foreign nationals through other legislation. In the case of the EU member countries these include the free movement of labour within the union – except for the accession states that have been discriminated against by their new partners. Domestic political factors also weigh here, including the willingness or otherwise of government to tackle concerns of host communities about the adequacy of social provision, to engage in debate over the cultural impact of migration and immigration, and to combat xenophobia.

The second strand is the enforcement of these parameters. This is the resourcing and implementation of policy through border controls, raids on workplaces and communities, detention, prosecution and deportation, combating people smuggling and trafficking. The final strand is policing the employment of those officially or complicitly allowed to work, the operation of visa and permit conditions, monitoring of conditions at work and benefit claims, compliance with health and safety regulations, tax gathering. The contention of this chapter is that in the case of the British government – and, evidence suggests, others – these functions are being determined and enacted with incompetence, discrimination and cruelty that will only be deepened by planned initiatives.

Determination: colour coding migrant workers

Two government policies are set to racialise migrant labour in Britain. We have already seen how migrant labour is concentrated in low-income jobs. Sometimes the concentration is quite racially specific, as we saw in contract cleaning in London. Kalayaan reports employers frequently seeking female domestic workers from various Asian countries because they are considered to be good with children.

The 2007 accession of Bulgaria and Romania to the EU meant the British government had to decide whether to extend the same limited rights it had given to previous accession states or prevent access to the labour market for the several years permissible. It opted for the latter course.[1] Backing up the argument that quite enough migrants were coming into the country to fill actual and potential job vacancies – a point that divided industry opinion – were implicit characterisations of Bulgarians and Romanians as having criminal tendencies. These characterisations drew on EU concerns about government corruption and organised crime in those countries. Such stereotyping has already dogged Latin American migrant workers, who, according to the Latin American Workers' Association, suffer from characterisation as drug smugglers.

If some central Europeans are more welcome than others, what of everyone else? The government is pushing ahead with a 'points-based' system of access to the British labour market for non-EU citizens. While a primary reason given for the new system is a simplification of entry procedures, which is a worthy objective, the Command document putting the proposals before Parliament does not disguise the racial grounding of the enterprise. In brief, the new system establishes five categories of migrant. To enter a category a would-be migrant must score adequate points, which are awarded according to the assessed demands of the British economy. We can ignore the student and youth mobility categories. Of the three remaining, one comprises highly skilled individuals who the government wants to attract lest they go elsewhere. Such high-value individuals do not require a job in advance and will be encouraged to settle. The second category comprises skilled people coming to fill specific job vacancies. They too, in the jargon of the document, will have a route to settlement. The third is defined as 'limited numbers of low skilled workers needed to fill specific temporary labour shortages'.[2] By contrast with categories one and two:

> Those entering the country under Tiers 3–5 are however entering under temporary categories where the expectation is that people will return home at the end of their stay in the UK. As such, they should not be able to apply for settlement, and apart from students in Tier 4, some of whom we will want to attract into the UK workforce, will also not be permitted to switch into other Tiers.[3]

The document is, then, admirably candid. Those with highly marketable skills may come and settle whether they have a job offer or not. Those with slightly less valuable credentials may come and stay as long as they have a job in place on arrival. Overseas students may be encouraged to stay if they look likely to be profitable after their studies are complete. By contrast, those seeking low-skilled jobs (which, in the case of migrant workers, by no means indicates low-skilled individuals) are quite explicitly treated as a stopgap reservoir of labour to be imported and returned home to order, with no hope or expectation of remaining.

What permits this is the accession of the central European countries to the EU. Henceforth, Europeans receive preference for even the worst jobs in Britain:

> With an expanded European Union there is an accessible and mobile workforce already contributing to our growing economy, closing many gaps experienced by employers. In a changing environment where our European commitments provide many opportunities for the UK to benefit from this new source of labour, it is right that we look again at migration to the UK as a whole. Our starting point is that employers should look first to recruit from the UK and the expanded EU before recruiting migrants from outside the EU.[4]

In case that was not clear enough, we read further on:

> The Five Year Strategy set out that we would phase out low-skilled migration in response to numbers of workers available from the newly enlarged EU, and that the only low-skilled routes which remained would be quota-based, operator-led, time-limited, subject to review, and only from countries with which the UK has effective returns arrangements. Any new routes will be based on identifications of temporary shortages by the Skills Advisory Board.[5]

The plan creates classes of workers with differing rights. According to the demands of British employers, workers may be categorised in one class or another, converting 'rights' into incentives that may be granted or withdrawn. And overlaying this, for third-tier workers, will be the principle that they – principally people from developing countries – will be a lesser class set apart from their European co-workers.

Those few workers who will be admitted for low-skilled jobs from outside of the EU will be tightly controlled once they arrive and treated as potential perpetrators of 'immigration crime'. The responsibilities of employers to police workers while they are in the country will be increased with tightened requirements to inform the authorities if they leave jobs. Compulsory remittances, a requirement to possess return tickets, and holding of biometric data are all under consideration.[6] The last provision ties in with the intention to force identity cards on foreign nationals before they are introduced for locals. This raises the spectre of further police powers to stop and search anyone with a dark skin or a foreign accent.

The Joint Council for the Welfare of Immigrants (JCWI) was damning in its criticism of the plan, arguing it lacked a sense of the rights of workers, which were viewed 'as factors which can be manipulated by the authorities to reduce the attractiveness of residence in the UK and to assert greater control over their presence in the workplace and the community'.[7] The inability of workers to switch employer will militate towards abusive and forced labour, the JCWI said, because poor workers will have made large investments in their migration which they will have to recoup before returning home, giving them little option but to put up with whatever conditions are imposed. In effect, the labour will be bonded. That third-tier workers will have no right to be joined by family members is in contravention of basic human rights enshrined in international labour conventions, the JCWI states.

The points-based system does not include migrant domestic workers, but the government is changing the rules here also to remove their rights in line with those affected by the scheme. The proposals roll back the gains made in 1998 when, in response to the outcry over reports of gross physical and psychological abuse, workers were permitted to change employer. That right will be removed so workers will be tied to potentially abusive employers by changing their status to that of business visitor. Their visas will last only six months instead of twelve and employers' responsibility for their status will be increased. Kalayaan argues that these measures will lead to trafficking, more widespread abuse, and the driving underground of more workers.[8]

Experience shows that the more managed, restricted and hedged about with regulatory barbed wire migrant labour is, the less control the authorities actually have over it. If the law prevents people from earning a living through formal channels, they will do so through informal channels. Just as its predecessors have done, the points-based system will criminalise workers. This will constitute a failure of the stated objective of controlling migration more effectively.

Enforcement – arbitrary, costly, ineffective

It is widely agreed that borders cannot be sealed completely against those who wish to enter and work without permission. That much is evident from the Canary Islands to the Mexican border, where financial cost, deportation and death have not slowed the flow of migrants. More mundanely, as a recent EU document noted of 2004 accession-state workers:

> Those countries which did not impose restrictions after May 2004 enjoyed strong economic growth, a fall in unemployment and an increase in employment, while in the other countries there were higher levels of undeclared work and bogus self-employment. According to the report, migratory flows cannot be regulated by national restrictions but depend instead on factors related to supply and demand.[9]

In other words, Polish and Lithuanian and Czech and Slovak and other central European workers found work abroad where it was available, irrespective of the policies of the host governments in 2004, just as they had done for years before (as noted earlier, 100,000 Polish workers were already in Britain when they signed up under the Worker Registration Scheme).

With hundreds of thousands of foreign students and millions of tourists entering a country like Britain every year, it is impossible to forecast who will overstay or work in a London Soho restaurant rather than studying in one of the language schools a few blocks away in Tottenham Court Road. The profits to be made from smuggling guarantee that people will continue to enter in the back of lorries or by cargo ship or light aircraft. False passports are available in capital cities throughout the world, so the unwelcome Brazilian is transformed for a price into the welcomed Portuguese, and once in Britain a few tens of pounds secures a National Insurance number. Even after the crackdown on asylum seekers – a term once evoking sympathy but now used to provoke suspicion and antipathy – it is difficult to deport someone without papers or admitted origin; so, with detention centres full to bursting and deportation centres prone to rioting,[10] the detained are released on bail to disappear.

The issue for the enforcers is clearly one of cost–benefit analysis, of how much effort and expense are to be used up limiting the inflow and ejecting a proportion of those who make it in. With the estimate of up to 570,000 undocumented people in Britain and some 50,000 being detained for expulsion, deportation looks less effective than just leaving people alone and saving the money given that 'almost half (46 per cent) of all overseas-born immigrants left the UK within five years of arrival between 1981 and 2002'.[11]

For the sake of populist posture the undocumented are harried to give the appearance that politicians are doing something. This book has cited examples of the workplace raid – the two

Bolivians and their fellow workers who were told they were off to work for a large high-street chain but were handed over to the immigration authorities; cleaners deported without being able to make arrangements for their children or possessions; hotel workers seeing their replacements waiting to start work as they were taken away by the authorities. Tellingly, in these and other cases reported by trade-union officials, the suspicion has been that civil servants and employers or labour providers have colluded, the one notching up a successful trawl and the other avoiding prosecution. In the construction industry, the assumption is that sites will receive tip-offs prior to raids, again, anecdotally at any rate, indicating collusion between officials and industry, allowing business to continue pretty much undisturbed.

The ongoing purge of asylum seekers saw them humiliated by a voucher system that forced them to exchange tokens for food. When that was scrapped in 2002 it was replaced with paltry cash payments far below the welfare benefits available to nationals. In the same year, the right of asylum seekers to seek work six months after their arrival was revoked and, in effect, replaced with a 12 month delay, this despite the fact that many asylum seekers are qualified in professions for which Britain has a shortage. Then began the campaign to remove as many asylum seekers as possible as quickly as possible. So in May 2006, Home Office Minister Liam Byrne bragged:

> The figures published today show that in February we met our target of removing more failed asylum seekers than there were suspected unfounded claims and sustained this during March. This is a significant achievement and is a result of our determined efforts to ensure those who have no right to remain in the UK are returned home.[12]

Then hundreds more policemen were switched to immigration control tasks.[13] With opportunities for legal employment closed

down and welfare benefits limited to pitiful amounts, little wonder
some asylum seekers start unauthorised working. Some women
end up moving into prostitution.

Notionally, there have long been stiff penalties in the UK for
employing undocumented workers, although prosecutions have been
few and far between. But recently the rhetoric has been stepped
up with the enactment of gangmaster licensing legislation and the
government's declaration that Bulgarians' and Romanians' access
to Britain would be restricted; employers taking on illegal workers
could expect a hefty fine if caught. Just as 2004 accession-state
workers evaded the restrictions on moving to earlier EU member
countries that sought to limit their access, so Bulgarians and Romanians and employers will no doubt find ways around these regulations. But damage is being done elsewhere in the meantime. Émigré
Chinese communities are renowned for their self-sufficiency, but
this has been undermined by fear of accusations of aiding undocumented migrants. Jabez Lam, the community worker quoted
earlier, says that where in the past a homeless migrant might find
lodgings and employment in the community, now there is wariness
and an erosion of solidarity. In 2006, prison sentences were handed
down to a couple found to be harbouring and employing four undocumented workers at a Chinese restaurant in Humberside.[14] If a
casual job in a restaurant with a place to sleep is not available, the
pull is towards the more questionable activities of the gangs that
Father Eddie Wu sees as a survival mechanism for many.[15]

Domestic workers escaping abusive employers and migrant
prostitutes evading violence, including trafficking, are generally
not able to claim housing benefit in Britain but clearly can be
in urgent need of accommodation. There are refuges for women
throughout the country but they are funded by the housing benefit
their tenants bring in. Thus, women may be turned away from the
one place where they might expect the door to be open. Amid a

major national police operation against the trafficking of women for prostitution, a single oversubscribed state-funded hostel was available to women said to be rescued. This further victimisation of the victim exemplifies the broader hypocrisy of a government strong on the rhetoric of helping victims of trafficking but whose concept of practical assistance frequently amounts to little more than deportation. As 2006 came to a close, the British government was still refusing to sign the Council of Europe Convention on Action Against Trafficking in Human Beings. The convention extends protection for victims of trafficking beyond those trafficked for sex to those trafficked for all forced labour and services whether transnationally or domestically.

Cold-hearted bureaucracy or incompetence? There is more to it than either of these explanations. Government conducts two parallel discourses around undocumented migrants. They become victims or villains as it suits. According to the police, Operation Pentameter freed over 80 women from forced prostitution (a number strongly contested by the English Collective of Prostitutes) but also detained 100 other women as illegal immigrants. For the ECP, Pentameter was another cover for a crackdown on migrant prostitutes, the vast majority of whom have not been trafficked, while daily violence against prostitutes gets little priority.

Jabez Lam of Min Quan, the Chinese community organisation, argues that government wheels out the notion that undocumented workers are victims of trafficking when it suits, as in the case of the 58 who died in the back of the lorry entering Britain. This, he argues, like the response to the cockle pickers' deaths at Morecambe Bay, serves to distract from the fact that government immigration and asylum policy created the circumstances that led to the tragedies.

In this discourse, the undocumented are presented as victims of crime, where in fact the overwhelming majority are (relatively) free agents who have actively decided to run the risks and incur the costs (and severe penalties for non-payment) of being smuggled into a destination of their choice.

The other discourse is the flip side of the coin. Here the undocumented migrant is the villain not the victim. The smuggled and the smuggler are conflated as a joint danger. A catch-all category of 'immigration crime' enables ministers and officials to slide from reference to failed asylum seekers to smuggling gangs to undocumented migrants in a single press release. Unveiling a 25 per cent rise in the number of immigration officers, it opens with the announcement of a new record number of deportations of refused asylum applicants. Then, Home Secretary John Reid and the head of the Serious Organised Crime Agency talk tough about 'The criminals behind organised immigration crime [who] are motivated by profit and treat people purely as commodities', causing 'direct harm to individuals, communities and businesses in the UK'. Finally, immigration minister Liam Byrne sums the initiative up as:

> the first part of our response; how we are going to use a doubling of resources to crack down on immigration crime … the next step in a comprehensive strategy, to transform enforcement of the immigration system in the UK and improve IND's ability to detect, detain and remove illegal immigrants.[16]

To cap it all, in early 2007 Reid came out with radical proposals to split his cumbersome department, creating a new National Security ministry responsible for counter-terrorism, border controls, the police and immigration.[17] Quite overtly, one of the most senior members of government associated the inflow of people into the UK not with employment law, community relations, or social provision but with crime and terror, with threats to the nation rather than benefits to the economy and society.

Policing: rights come second

The policing of migrant labour employment is the third strand of policy. Here there are petty stupidities of policy such as the government announcement that it would begin charging migrant workers for English language classes.[18] Job Centres, police stations, the tax credit agency are routinely accused of casual racism towards migrants. While penny-pinching in a government department, acerbic remarks from petty officials and the apathy of desk officers may be considered unfortunate, the inadequacies of major policy regarding migrant labour demonstrates fundamental flaws in the policing of employment.

The Worker Registration Scheme, as explained in Chapter 1, requires 2004 accession-state nationals wishing to be employed in Britain (those claiming to be self-employed are exempt) to pay a registration fee and provide a letter of accreditation from an employer. The scheme can run until 2011 under EU arrangements. Its main intention, according to Dee Coombes, a specialist advice worker in Liverpool, was to prevent accession-state nationals from accessing state benefits, particularly housing benefits and access to local authority housing. This has been a boon to private landlords. It may have prevented competition between local people and migrants for council-owned accommodation but it has facilitated the overcrowding and overcharging imposed by some landlords (who are often also labour providers) and led to concern over conversion of houses into multi-occupancy dwellings. Because they cannot claim housing benefit, accession-state workers, like domestic workers, often cannot even turn to hostels for the homeless if they lose their accommodation.

After one year of continuous employment, workers registered under the scheme become entitled to the same rights as other EU citizens. But there is a catch. A period of non-employment of over thirty days puts the clock back to the start, the time in work already accrued counts for nothing, and a new registration fee must be found by workers, 97 per cent of whom are in low-paid and low-skill jobs. A change of job requires re-registration and another payment.

Dee Coombes says some employment agencies are known to charge administration fees for posting registration forms to the Home Office or to sit on forms so they can be sent off in large batches so workers do not know accurately when their one-year period has commenced. Others are reported to lay off workers just before the twelve months is up in order to prevent them from moving on. One report found evidence that some employers were not registering workers, meaning they would not accrue full EU rights.[19]

The second important piece of legislation affecting migrant workers is the Gangmaster Licensing Act of 2006. Trade unions had been campaigning for a clampdown on gangmastering for fifty years. When the Labour government was elected in 1997 there were high hopes of early legislation, but these were soon dashed by an administration that had adopted the business lobby's preference for self-regulation.

There was a move towards self-regulation by labour providers who wanted to distance themselves from the more visibly exploitative end of the business. At the same time the supermarkets began to feel the pressure of public and political criticism of the devastating effects of their ruthlessness on small businesses and high-street retailers. The Association of Labour Providers was established and the Ethical Trading Initiative (which counts trade unions, corporations and trade associations among its members) set up the Temporary Labour Working Group. That group devised and introduced an audit system for labour providers.

With the outcry over the deaths of the cockle pickers in More-cambe Bay, the government had to be seen to act, so the Gangmaster Licensing Act was brought into effect. On examination the Act looks like a kneejerk reaction rather than a serious attempt to eradicate gross exploitation. In an astounding indication of complacency, laziness or effective complicity with exploitative practices, the Act only covers labour providers in agriculture and shellfish harvesting. Indeed, long was the consultation and evident was the lack of enthusiasm in some government department offices before even food packing and processing operations were included. Among the exclusions are those providing labour to food retailers and wholesalers or caterers. Also, the short-term transfer of labour from farm to farm does not require a licence.

From the start the legislation was overseen by the agriculture department and its remit matches that of the department rather than reaching across into parts of the economy dealt with by the Department for Trade and Industry. But, increasingly, labour providers operate across sectors. Workers who start out on a farm may be moved to a meat-packing plant and then on to a contract cleaning job. As they do so, ludicrously, they slip in and out of the protection the Act is supposed to provide.

To be awarded a licence an applicant must abide by a long list of worthy conditions from payment of the minimum wage, including holiday pay, to not making illegal deductions, providing proper payslips to not putting workers into debt bondage and not using intimidation to control them or taking possession of passports.

Some of the most excoriating criticism of the Act has come from Mark Boleat, a consultant to trade associations who was chairman of the Association of Labour Providers for two years until mid-2006.[20] He says the drafters of the legislation simply do not understand how the employment system works. The Act is misnamed, he says, as it covers employment agencies while many gangmasters fall outside of its terms. Many gangmasters escape it because of its sectoral specificity or because they operate outside the law anyway. (In April 2007 the government was pressed into saying it would review the scope of the Act after embarrassing TV news stories about abuses. Such pious statements of concern were reactive, not proactive, and comprehensive action looked far from likely.)

Some labour users will believe they are dealing with an employment agency whereas under the terms of the Act the agency will be a gangmaster. They will unwittingly fall foul of the law if they use one that is unlicensed. Mark Boleat described the scope of the Act as 'rather like having a Dangerous Dogs Act that in practice covered cats and excluded most dogs'.[21] He admitted that 'There are crooks among our members' and that big labour providers with high-street offices sometimes act illegally. Compliance with the Act will largely be a matter of presentation and record keeping. Compulsory deductions for transport have been made illegal, so labour providers will simply say use of the transport is optional although no alternative will be available. Among his conclusions are that the Act will be of little benefit to workers, will fail to help recoup the £100 million a year the government believes it loses from tax evasion by rogue labour providers, while the licence fees will encourage bad operators to shift to other sectors and abuse workers there instead while small operators will be tempted to evade the system because of the costs of licensing and of compliance.

Small-scale labour providers in rural areas may only operate for a few months a year, perhaps as a sideline to other business. They may simply shut up shop, conceivably producing local labour shortages. Or farmers may decide to source their own labour from abroad, doing so legally or illegally and with the possibility of gross exploitation being more hidden because the workers may be entirely confined to isolated farms.

When it comes to the most abusive gangmasters, those using irregular and bonded labour, the Act is an irrelevance because they are operating well outside pre-existing laws:

> They do not have formal contracts with the workers they supply and indeed it would be difficult to prove they were actually supplying the workers in a way which would bring them within the Act. Typically, an illegal gangmaster will bring people into the country who are not entitled to be here, taking money from the workers for arranging this, and then there will be informal and undocumented arrangements for the workers to be housed and to be employed. The workers are in the country illegally, and are occupying housing that does not meet legal requirements, are themselves evading tax and are working for people who are evading tax.[22]

Then, for all the huffing and puffing about penalties, many labour providers and the employers who use them will look at the statistics and draw their own conclusions: between 1998 and 2004, just seventeen employers were successfully prosecuted for illegally employing migrants under the amended 1996 Asylum and Immigration Act. More than half received fines of less than £700, with four fined the maximum of £5,000.[23] Even though the maximum penalty for operating without a gangmaster licence is a more sobering ten years in prison, precedent suggests that those breaking the law stand little chance of being caught and less chance of suffering more than a slap on wrist.

In all three policy strands the British government is at best inept and at worst wilfully negligent of the welfare of migrant workers, documented and undocumented. The enforcement of entry rules is impossible and enforcement measures do no more than reduce the net number of undocumented workers in the country. The technical fix of biometric identity documents could only work in a regime where regular and systematic checking of documentation was in operation and if the technology worked.

The first condition would not only be resource-intensive, it would also constitute a frontal assault on civil liberties. And, like all technological fixes, biometric IDs will solve little, and may simply create new problems – biometric passports have already been hacked into using equipment costing no more than $200.[24] Initiatives against people trafficking become entangled with the very different issue of people smuggling, and the rhetoric against the evil of trafficking is not matched by the failure to provide legal status or support for victims. Indeed the government has chosen to promote a narrative in which migration is associated with law and order rather than rights. In this narrative, a few may be portrayed as victims but for the many the first questions demanded of them are not whether their workplace rights are being observed but what their immigration status is, whether they are correctly registered, how they arrived in the UK, and whether they should be allowed to remain.

No wonder, then, that the policing of employment fails to protect workers because it is not predicated on their rights and welfare. The Worker Registration Scheme is primarily a means to keep migrants out of social housing and off benefits for as long as possible. The gangmaster registration legislation was a knee-jerk reaction to popular outrage over Morecambe Bay and is not fit for its ostensible purpose. Even leaving aside questions about its effectiveness within agriculture and food processing, limiting it to that one sector is an invitation to extend abusive practices elsewhere. Enforcement and policing are necessarily weighted against the interests of migrant workers and ultimately local workers because of the thrust of the central policy of determination. There we see a government that is racialising its migrant employment practice and, at the same time, increasing controls over workers and the likelihood of gross exploitation.

Conclusion

The dependence of the global North on migrant labour increases with the ageing of populations in the rich world. Basic industries we rely on to feed us, house us, transport us and provide for our leisure time cannot function efficiently without workers from abroad. There is mounting evidence that the overall health of our economies, as measured by conventional economics, now relies on migrant labour to bolster growth rates and temper inflation and interest rates. The benefits are reaped directly by employers propping up margins and guarding profits against local and global competition and liberalised trade practices. Much of the general population also benefits indirectly through low prices for goods and services. These prices are reliant in part on migrant labour working for low wage rates in low-status jobs or providing skills that host countries fail to train for. From the start, migrant labour is subsidised by the exporting countries where workers were raised and educated. Then it is exploited over and above the exploitation of the indigenous workforce. Employers describe this in terms of work ethic. They extol the virtues of migrants who will work long and anti-social hours without complaint. The other side of the coin is that migrants work such hours because they have signed away rights or because the very uncertainty of their hours and temporariness of their employment mean they will take what they can when it is available. 'Jobs on site are denoted by hat colour. The Portuguese – along with the smaller cohorts of Asian, African and east European migrant workers – are almost invariably "yellow hats", or basic workers, paid a little over £200 a week.'[1] This is where the continuum of super-exploitation begins, with corralling of migrants into the lowest-paid, lowest-status jobs, but it runs all the way through to the manufactured indebtedness that turns a job into bonded labour or the intimidation that creates forced labour, modern-day slavery for modern-day economies. Here, right in the heart of our societies, are workers no less abused by 'our' industries than are the labourers in Southeast Asian textile mills and silicon-chip plants who provide us with jeans sold in supermarkets for a pittance and ever cheaper computers. The difference is that in the case of the migrant the work cannot be taken to the worker, so the worker is taken to the work. The super-exploitation of migrant workers by the global North demands a response just as much as the super-exploitation in overseas factories. It demands a response that breaks free of the victim–villain dichotomy posed by UK government discourse, consumed and regurgitated by media outlets that can sell corpses in trucks, snakehead gangs, threats to 'our' jobs, and trafficked women, but are not so interested in the rights of workers propping up British agriculture, construction, hospitality or commercialised sex.

In Britain the government increasingly treats migrant workers as a factor of production, the supply of which is to be regulated in accordance with employers' requirements and at the lowest possible cost. Rights are not high on the agenda. So, it has been left to the labour movement and other non-governmental organisations to defend migrant workers. Dedication, sometimes bravery, can be seen in the work of many union officials, from workplace organisers to regional officials. Industrial disputes involving migrant workforces are being given more and more prominence in union publications. Polish or Portuguese speakers – often migrants themselves – are now regularly employed in areas where there is concentration of migrants. Literature about workplace rights is being produced in the languages of migrant workers. The Polish trade-union federation Solidarnosc has a presence in Britain, and British unions have been to central Europe to establish lines of communication with potential migrants before they set off. There are moves towards establishing labour movement passports that would ensure migrant workers came under union protection on arrival at their destination. Very importantly, there is a general refusal to discriminate between documented and undocumented workers.

At the trade-union leadership level, speeches decrying the exploitation of migrants are common. The Trades Union Congress, the federation of British unions, usefully produced a report on vulnerable workers, including agency workers, casual workers, homeworkers and migrants.[2] One in five workers could be classed as vulnerable, it said. The approach of the document was useful precisely because it rolled migrant workers in with others rather than isolating them. Migrant workers, of course, often fall into one or more of the other categories, just as gross exploitation may be more common to but is not exclusive to migrants. And that is crucial. Employers determined to defend or increase their margins will use whatever labour, machinery or location proves cheapest and, of course, will substitute one of these factors for another when it suits, replacing workers with machines or vice versa or moving to a lower-cost country.

Some union organisers and some migrant community workers express the concern that for all the good work that is being done at some levels in some unions, there remains a reluctance to provide the resources needed to defend migrant workers. A worker with one migrant community worried that trade-union lawyers shied away from cases involving migrants. A trade-union official spoke of the need to spend time educating British members before devoting too many resources to migrant workers in case the local membership became resentful.

As Chapter 3, on the impact of migration, attempted to show, the effect of an influx of migrant workers on indigenous employment (and wages) is not straightforward. It depends on the sector, perhaps the segment of the sector, or even the company. It also depends on the time frame and circumstances taken into account. Given these complexities, the suspicion expressed by Robert Rowthorn that 'Large-scale immigration of unskilled people may be beneficial for urban elites who enjoy the benefits of cheap servants, restaurants and the like, but it is not to the economic advantage of those who have to compete with these immigrants'[3] is reasonable and sometimes well founded.

But this should be no dilemma for the labour movement. Migrant workers are a permanent element of the workforce. If they are being used to drive down wages and conditions or their cheapness is spurring employers to substitute them for local workers, that is all the more reason to devote time, effort and solidarity to defending them. If there is competition between migrants and local workers for jobs, there are only two ways in which the terms of competition will be equalised: one is by depressing the wages and conditions of the locals, and the other is by raising the wages and conditions of migrants. Clearly the latter is the path for the labour movement, which is not to say it is easy to achieve. The more isolated and exploited workers are, the more difficult it is for them to organise. When there are difficulties of language, instructions from employers not to fraternise, where workers are regularly replaced or work irregular hours, let alone when they are undocumented, the problems are even greater. Nonetheless, ingenuity is to be found in initiatives like the GMB's community branches, where workers are contacted through bars and churches and Internet cafés.

Beyond the specifics of local organisation, there need to be broader demands of government, demands that taken together would shift the trajectory of migrant labour policy. I conclude with a provisional list.

- The absurdity and cruelty of criminalising undocumented workers must end. Only by making their status regular (as has frequently been done in, say, France, Spain and Italy) can their super-exploitation be ended so they can compete on equal terms with other workers and have access to law. At the same time, the public purse will be swelled by tax payments they currently do not make and by savings on the doomed drive to hunt them to extinction.

- An increase in immigration raids on workplaces while health and safety inspectorate posts are being cut exemplifies misplaced priorities. Ending the criminalisation of undocumented workers would free up resources that must be redirected to ensuring workers' rights are respected – more health and safety inspections and local inspectors monitoring employment practices. At the same time, regulation of labour providers needs to be reviewed. If it can be made fit for purpose, the amended version must cover all sectors and all labour providers.

- The most grossly exploited of migrants – the trafficked and others suffering forced labour – must be granted legal status where they lack it and adequate support. Traffickers must be punished, but countering trafficking must not be a cover for immigration raids.

- The racialisation of entry to Britain for low-skilled work must be opposed. Not only is it morally offensive but through the points-based entry system it threatens to create new distinctions and cleavages within individual workplaces and society at large, openly sanctioning an underclass of tightly controlled temporary workers with limited rights and high vulnerability to forced labour. More specifically, the rolling back of rights of highly vulnerable domestic workers alongside the introduction of the points-based system should be rejected loudly.

- A proportion of tax payments made by migrant workers should be earmarked for use in areas where there is a large migrant population. Investment in bilingual teaching staff, refurbishment of housing stock, additional funds for the health authority would reduce potential friction between local people, worried about pressure on scarce resources, and migrant workers. It would constitute concrete proof of the economic benefits of hosting migrant workers and would give the latter a sense of participation in the host community's affairs.

- The poaching of professional staff, particularly health workers, from developing countries is a scandal. Where they are recruited, the employer should, at minimum, pay for the cost of training a replacement, thus recognising that migration of skilled workers is not just a transfer of staff but a lost investment to the home country while the employer benefits from lower-cost training.

- The labour movement must build on work done so far to support migrant workers. The forceful argument must be made that by ensuring vulnerable groups of workers, of which migrant workers are one, do not work excessive hours in poor conditions for unacceptable wages, the labour movement is lifting the floor for all workers and opposing employers' attempts to lower it. Organising migrant workers poses obvious problems. Overcoming these will require investment of trade-union time, money and initiative, but the payback will be significant. Trade unions will experiment with new ways of working in the community, will expand international links and information gathering, and strengthen workplace organisation, undermining attempts to divide and rule employees.

These proposals are modest. They draw on no more than basic precepts of the labour movement that all workers are paid equally in wages and respect, that a worker's origin or immigration status is not manipulated by employers in order to discriminate, and that government does not collude in such discrimination. But despite their modesty, these proposals (with local variations) promoted across the global North constitute a starting point for an international labour response to capital's version of globalisation.

Notes

Introduction

1. Ignacio Ramonet, *Manière de voir*, editorial, Paris, January–February 2007, p. 4.
2. Ibid., p. 5.
3. United Nations Conference on Trade and Development, *World Investment Report 2006 – Overview*, Geneva, 2006, pp. 1–11.
4. Federal Reserve Bank of Dallas, *Southwest Economy*, September–October 2003, www.dallasfed.org/research/swe/2003/swe0305a.html.
5. Klara Skrivankova, *Trafficking for Forced Labour – UK Country Report*, Anti-Slavery International, London, 2006, p. 8.
6. Kevin Bales, *Disposable People: New Slavery in the Global Economy'*, University of California Press, Berkeley, 2004, p. 25.
7. www.ilo.org/dyn/declaris/declarationweb.issueshome?var_language= EN.
8. Answer given to questioner at a seminar organised by the trade union Unison in London, 12 May 2006.

Chapter 1

1. *El País*, Madrid, 3 November 2005.
2. *El País*, Madrid, 5 October 2005.
3. *El País*, Madrid, 13 October 2005.
4. *Guardian*, London, 22 September 2005.
5. *El País*, Madrid, 29 September 2005.

6. 'Division over Bush Migrant Plan', http://news.bbc.co.uk/1/hi/world/americas/4986316.stm, 16 May 2006.
7. http://newstandardnews.net/content/index.cfm/items/1692.
8. www.msnbc.msn.com/id/7725470/.
9. Wayne Cornelius, 'Impacts of Border Enforcement on Unauthorised Mexican Migration to the United States', SSRC, September 2006, http://borderbattles.ssrc.org/Cornelius/.
10. *El Periódico*, Barcelona, 20 August 2006.
11. *El País*, Madrid, 6 September 2006.
12. http://news.bbc.co.uk/1/hi/world/africa/5383080.stm.
13. *El Periódico*, Barcelona, 20 August 2006.
14. *El Periódico*, Barcelona, 24 August 2006.
15. *Evening Standard*, London, 7 September 2006.
16. Home Office press release, London, 22 August 2006.
17. *Daily Express*, London, 18 August 2006.
18. *Sun*, London, 18 August 2006.
19. *Daily Telegraph*, London, 18 August 2006.
20. *Daily Telegraph*, London, 23 August 2006.
21. http://news.bbc.co.uk/1/hi/uk_politics/5119892.stm.
22. A. Green, D. Owen and R. Wilson, *Changing Patterns of Employment by Ethnic Group and for Migrant Workers*, Warwick Institute for Employment Research, November 2005, p. 81.
23. Jonathon Moses, *International Migration: Globalisation's Last Frontier*, Zed Books, London, 2006, p. 13.
24. www.iom.int/jahia/page8.html.
25. Patrick Taran and Gloria Moreno-Fontes Chammartin, *Getting at the Roots: Stopping Exploitation of Migrant Workers by Organised Crime*, Perspectives on Migration, ILO, Geneva, 2003, pp. 3–4.
26. Interviews with Jabez Lam of community group Min Quan, and with Father Eddie Wu, London 2006.
27. http://news.bbc.co.uk/1/hi/uk/4257397.stm.
28. Cornelius, 'Impacts of Border Enforcement'.
29. Ibid.
30. Alain Morice, 'L'utilitarisme migratoire en question', ATTAC France, 10 December 2002, www.france.attac.org/spip.php?article1495.
31. Figures provided by Jabez Lam of Min Quan in an interview.
32. Cornelius, 'Impacts of Border Enforcement'.
33. *Le Monde Diplomatique*, Paris, September 2006.
34. *Financial Times*, London, 12 July 2004.
35. Morice, 'L'utilitarisme migratoire en question'.
36. John Berger and Jean Mohr, *A Seventh Man*, Granta Books, London, 1989, pp. 17–18.
37. Gunter Walraff, 'I Am the Law', in *Walraff: The Undesirable Journalist*,

Pluto Press, London, 1978, p. 111.

38. Jeffrey Passel, *The Size and Characteristics of the Unauthorized Migrant Population in the US: Estimates Based on the March 2006 Current Population Survey*, Pew Hispanic Center, Washington DC, 7 March 2006, p. 1.

39. Cornelius, 'Impacts of Border Enforcement'.

40. Taran and Moreno-Fontes Chammartin, *Getting at the Roots*, p. 4.

41. Interview with workers at the Day Mer community organisation, London, 2006.

42. Berger and Mohr, *A Seventh Man*, p. 58.

43. Ibid., p. 64.

44. Ibid., p. 69.

45. Taran and Moreno-Fontes Chammartin, *Getting at the Roots*, p. 1.

46. Moses, *International Migration*, ch. 6.

47. www.elpais.es, 28 August 2006.

48. Morice, 'L'utilitarisme migratoire en question'.

49. Patrick Taran and Eduardo Geronimi, *Globalisation, Labour and Migration: Protection is Paramount*, Perspectives on Migration, ILO, Geneva, 2003, p. 6.

50. Passel, *The Size and Characteristics of the Unauthorized Migrant Population in the US*, p. 2.

51. Ibid., p. i.

52. ITEM Club Special Report, *Finding Our Potential*, Ernst & Young, London, September 2006, p. 4.

53. OECD, *International Migration Outlook*, Paris, 2006, p. 16.

54. Ibid., p. 22.

55. Ibid., p. 21.

56. John Sutton, 'Opening the Floodgates', Workers Online, April 2006, http://workers.labor.net.au/features/200604/c_historicalfeature_sutton.html.

57. See, for example, *Temporary Migrant Workers: The Challenge to the AMIEU*, www.amieu.asn.au/pages.php?recid=120.

58. Passel, *The Size and Characteristics of the Unauthorized Migrant Population in the US*, p. ii.

59. OECD, *International Migration Outlook*, p. 233.

60. Ibid., p. 248.

61. Ibid., p. 274.

62. Here I am following the methodology of Sally Dench et al., *Employers' Use of Migrant Labour (Main Report)*, Home Office Online Report, London, April 2006.

63. Home Office press release, 22 August 2006.

64. Ibid.

65. *Irregular Migration in the UK*, IPPR, London, 2006, p. 9.

66. John Salt and Jane Millar, *Foreign Labour in the United Kingdom: Current*

Patterns and Trends, Office for National Statistics, London, October 2006.

67. Home Office, *Accession Monitoring Report: May 2004–June 2006*, HMSO, London, 22 August 2006, p. 9.
68. OECD, *International Migration Outlook*, p. 248.
69. Home Office, *Accession Monitoring Report*, p. 12.
70. Newsnight, BBC 2, 6 July 2006.
71. *Mail on Sunday*, London, 3 December 2006.
72. Dench et al., *Employers' Use of Migrant Labour*, p. 15.
73. Home Office, *Accession Monitoring Report*, pp. 18–19.

Chapter 2

1. Charalambos Kasimis, *Migrants in the Rural Economies of Greece and Southern Europe*, Migration Policy Institute, 1 October 2005, www.migration-information.org/Feature/display.cfm?id=337.
2. Keith Hogart and Cristobal Mendoza, *African Immigrant Workers in Spanish Agriculture*, Center for Comparative Immigration Studies, University of California, San Diego, February 2000, p. 8.
3. E. Allasino et al., *Labour Market Discrimination against Migrant Workers in Italy*, ILO, Geneva, 2004, pp. 13–14.
4. US Department of Labor, *National Agricultural Workers Survey*, Washington DC, December 2005, ch. 1, p. 2.
5. See Peter Mares, *Seasonal Migrant Labour: A Boon for Australian Country Towns?*, La Trobe University, Melbourne, July 2005.
6. Kasimis, *Migrants in the Rural Economies of Greece and Southern Europe*.
7. Claudia Schneider and Deborah Holman, *A Profile of Migrant Workers in the Breckland Area*, Anglia Polytechnic University, Cambridge, July 2005, p. 13.
8. Home Office, *Accession Monitoring Report: May 2004–June 2006*, HMSO, London, 22 August 2006, p. 13.
9. Ibid., p. 14.
10. Ibid., p. 17.
11. Precision Prospecting, *Temporary Workers in UK Agriculture and Horticulture: A Study of Employment Practices in the Agriculture and Horticulture Industry and Co-located Packhouse and Primary Food Processing Sectors*, Framlingham, 2005, p. 11.
12. Ibid., p. 14.
13. Ibid., p. 17.
14. Corporate Watch, www.corporatewatch.org.uk/?lid=800#mirror.
15. Compass Group preliminary results for 2006, p. 3, www.compass-group.com/NR/rdonlyres/176ced11–a1e2–4c4d–9787–5eeea0239807/0/final-

versionmainpressrelease.pdf.

16. Precision Prospecting, *Temporary Workers in UK Agriculture and Horticulture*, pp. 21–2.

17. *Agriculture in the United Kingdom*, Defra, London, 2005, ch. 2, p. 14.

18. Ibid.

19. See Hogart and Mendoza, *African Immigrant Workers in Spanish Agriculture*, and Kasimis, *Migrants in the Rural Economies of Greece and Southern Europe*, for example.

20. Mares, *Seasonal Migrant Labour.*

21. Precision Prospecting, *Temporary Workers in UK Agriculture and Horticulture*, pp. 21–22.

22. www.defra.gov.uk/farm/working/gangmasters/pdf/research-study3.pdf.

23. Alain Morice, 'L'utilitarisme migratoire en question', ATTAC France, 10 December 2002, www.france.attac.org/spip.php?article1495.

24. Migrant Rights Centre Ireland, *Harvesting Justice: Mushroom Workers Call For Change*, Dublin, November 2006.

25. Karl Marx, *Capital*, Volume 1, Charles H. Kerr, Chicago, 1906, www.econlib.org/library/YPDBooks/Marx/mrxCpA25.html.

26. Answers to survey carried out for this book in May 2006.

27. Vale of Evesham Agriculture and Food Distribution Panel, *Report of the Panel – February 2004*, Wychavon District Council, 2004, p. 63.

28. For more detailed definitions, see www.defra.gov.uk/farm/working/gangmasters/faq.htm, and www.dti.gov.uk/files/file24248.pdf#search=%22Employment%20Agencies%20Act%201973%20definition%22.

29. *Environment, Food and Rural Affairs: Fourteenth Report*, House of Commons, London, 2003, www.publications.parliament.uk/pa/cm200203/cmselect/cmenvfru/691/69102.htm.

30. *Nowhere to Turn: CAB Evidence on the Exploitation of Migrant Workers*, Citizens' Advice Bureau, London, 2004, p. 5.

31. Observation appended to survey of bureaux carried out in May 2006 for this book.

32. Precision Prospecting, *Temporary Workers in UK Agriculture and Horticulture*, p. 11.

33. Allasino et al., *Labour Market Discrimination against Migrant Workers in Italy*, p. 14.

34. *Le Monde Diplomatique*, Paris, June 2005.

35. Mares, *Seasonal Migrant Labour.*

36. Philip Martin, *California's Farm Labor Market: Executive Summary*, California Institute for Rural Studies, Working Paper 4, 1989.

37. *Western Mail*, Cardiff, 16 September 2006.

38. www.telegraph.co.uk/news/main.jhtml?xml=/news/2006/07/15/nstrawbs15.xml.

39. *Guardian*, 15 February 2006.
40. *Observer*, 15 February 2004.
41. http://news.bbc.co.uk/1/hi/uk/3223560.stm.
42. http://news.bbc.co.uk/1/hi/england/lancashire/4851194.stm.
43. Hsiao-Hung Pai, 'Migrant Labour: The Unheard Story', www.open-democracy.net, 2 February 2006.
44. *T&G Record*, November/December 2005.
45. Free translation by author from text written by Ernesto.
46. I am grateful for the assistance of Andrew Large of the trade association CSSA for this information.
47. Cited in Sonia McKay et al., *Migrant Workers in England and Wales: An Assessment of Migrant Worker Health and Safety Risks*, Health and Safety Executive (HSE), London, 2006, p. 154.
48. Yara Evans et al., 'Making the City Work: Low Paid Employment in London', Queen Mary, University of London, November 2005, p. 4.
49. Morice, 'L'utilitarisme migratoire en question'.
50. Evans et al., 'Making the City Work', p. 5.
51. Interview with author, 25 May 2006.
52. Evans et al., 'Making the City Work', pp. 17, 21, 24.
53. *El Periódico*, Barcelona, 19 August 2006.
54. McKay et al., *Migrant Workers in England and Wales*, p. 154.
55. Author's interview with TGWU official, 11 May 2006.
56. Evans et al., 'Making the City Work', p. 24.
57. Information from interview with Unison organiser Maurice Sheehan, 16 October 2006.
58. Evans et al., 'Making the City Work', p. 15.
59. Interview with author, 7 July 2006.
60. Lyrics from 'Missing You', written by Christy Moore.
61. *The Labor Force Status of Short-term Unauthorized Workers*', Pew Hispanic Center, 13 April 2005, p. 2.
62. Allasino et al., *Labour Market Discrimination against Migrant Workers in Italy*, p. 10.
63. Terry Coleman, *The Railway Navvies*, Readers Union, London, 1966, p. 20.
64. Allasino et al., *Labour Market Discrimination against Migrant Workers in Italy*, p. 13.
65. Interview with author, 21 July 2006.
66. For example, *Contract Journal*, London, 11 October 2006.
67. Alex Balch and Andrew Geddes, *UK Migration Policy in Light of Sectoral Dynamic: The Case of the Construction Sector*, University of Liverpool, 2003, draft, p. 11.
68. Construction Industry Training Board press release, 5 June 2006.
69. Figure taken from Deloitte, *2005–2015 Construction Demand/Capacity Study*

(Full Report), London, June 2006, p. 56.

70. Ibid., p. 38.

71. National Engineering Construction Committee, *Social Dumping: A Crisis in the UK Engineering Construction Industry*', Amicus, Bromley, 2004.

72. Ian Fitzgerald, *Organising Migrant Workers in Construction: Experience from the North East of England*, Northern TUC, Newcastle-upon-Tyne, 2006, p. 16.

73. *Contract Journal*, London, 6 September 2006.

74. Bridget Anderson and Ben Rogaly, *Forced Labour and Migration to the UK*, TUC, London, 2005, p. 27.

75. Deloitte, *2005–2015 Construction Demand/Capacity Study*, pp. 6–7.

76. *Observer*, London, 8 October 2006.

77. McKay et al., *Migrant Workers in England and Wales*, p. 166.

78. 'Building Industry and Social Partners Call for Stricter Social Fraud Bill', European Industrial Relations Observatory, 7 June 2005, www.eiro.eurofound.eu.int/2005/06/inbrief/at0506201n.html.

79. Allasino et al., *Labour Market Discrimination against Migrant Workers in Italy*, p. 13.

80. Fitzgerald, *Organising Migrant Workers in Construction*, pp. 12–14.

81. Anderson and Rogaly, *Forced Labour and Migration to the UK*, p. 36.

82. www.thestar.co.za/index.php?fArticleId=3319090.

83. http://news.bbc.co.uk/1/hi/uk/975621.stm.

84. 'Regulatory Authorities to Stamp Out Illegal Work Practices Regarding Migrant Workers', *European Industrial Relations Observatory Online*, 9 November 2006, www.eiro.eurofound.eu.int/2006/09/articles/n006090039i.html.

85. 'Scandal over Illegal Employment of Posted Workers', European Industrial Relations Observatory Online, 27 June 2006, www.eiro.eurofound.eu.int/2006/05/articles/at0605019i.html.

86. *Migration News*, April 2005, University of California, Davis, http://migration.ucdavis.edu/mn/more.php?id=3097_0_4_0.

87. Balch and Geddes, *UK Migration Policy in Light of Sectoral Dynamic*, p. 6.

88. *Building Magazine*, London, 26 October 2001.

89. *PrintWeek*, London, 12 October 2006.

90. Information provided to the author.

91. TUC press release, London, 20 January 2006.

92. Irish Ferries preliminary statement of results for the year ended 31 December 2005, www.icg.ie/investor/announcements.

93. TUC press release, London, 20 January 2006.

94. RMT press release, London, 24 November 2006.

95. International Transport Workers' Federation, *Out of Sight, Out of Mind: Seafarers, Fishers and Human Rights*, London, 2006.

96. Information on cruise liner industry from International Transport Workers' Federation and War on Want, *Sweatships*, London, 2004.

97. *Shifting Sands: The Future of the Oil Industry*, 3i, London, September 2006, p. 17.

98. Contract issued by Offshore Manning Services (Cyprus) Ltd, 1 May 2005.

99. Amicus press release, London, 11 July 2006.

100. Document provided by OILC.

101. Interview with author, 15 September 2006.

102. Office for National Statistics, *Monthly Digest of Statistics*, London, January 2007, pp. 25, 33.

103. People 1st, *Skills Needs Assessment for the Hospitality, Leisure, Travel and Tourism Sector*, January 2006, p. 2.

104. 'Non-national Workers in the Hotels and Catering Sector', European Industrial Relations Observatory Online, 13 February 2006, http://www.eiro.eurofound.ie/2005/12/feature/es0512105f.html.

105. Telephone discussion with Martin Couchman of the British Hospitality Association, 5 September 2006.

106. People 1st, *Skills Needs Assessment*, p. 4.

107. www.manufacturingtalk.com/news/wok/wok104.html.

108. People 1st, *Skills Needs Assessment*, pp. 10–11.

109. 'Non-national Workers in the Hotels and Catering Sector', European Industrial Relations Observatory Online.

110. Press release of the Guild of Bangladeshi Restaurateurs, 2006, www.gbruk.org.uk/news13.htm.

111. Author's interview with Jabez Lam of Min Quan, 5 May 2006.

112. Interview with worker at the Day-Mer community project, 20 July 2006.

113. Monder Ram et al., *Employers and Illegal Migrant Workers in the Clothing and Restaurant Sectors*, Department of Trade and Industry, London, 2002, pp. 10–13.

114. Ibid., p. 21.

115. Monder Ram et al., *Informal Employment, Small Firms and the National Minimum Wages*, Low Pay Commission, London, September 2004, p. 28.

116. Ibid., p. 11.

117. Citizens' Advice Bureau, *Nowhere to Turn: CAB Evidence on the Exploitation of Migrant Workers*, London, 2004, pp. 11–12.

118. Ibid., pp. 9–10.

119. Klara Skrivankova, *Trafficking for Forced Labour: UK Country Report*, Anti-Slavery International, London, 2006, p.26.

120. Anderson and Rogaly, *Forced Labour and Migration to the UK*, p. 47.

121. Human Rights Watch, *Inside the House, Outside the Law: Abuse of Child Domestic Workers in Morocco*, London, 2005.

122. Human Rights Watch, *Maid to Order: Ending Abuses against Migrant Domestic Workers in Singapore*, 2005.

123. Bridget Anderson, *Doing the Dirty Work? The Global Politics of Domestic Labour*, Zed Books, London, 2000, p. 43.

124. Ibid., p. 44.

125. European Foundation for the Improvement of Living and Working Conditions, www.eiro.eurofound.eu.int/2002/05/feature/es0205206f. html.

126. European Foundation for the Improvement of Living and Working Conditions, www.eiro.eurofound.eu.int/2006/04/articles/es0604029i. html.

127. Allasino et al., *Labour Market Discrimination against Migrant Workers in Italy*, p. 5.

128. Ibid., p. 10.

129. Ibid., p. 11.

130. Ibid.

131. Ibid.

132. Ibid.

133. Paper delivered by Kalayaan community support worker Kate Roberts at the conference Twenty-first Century Slavery: Issues and Responses, Wilberforce Institute for the Study of Slavery and Emancipation, Hull, 23–24 November 2006.

134. *Annual Report April 2004–March 2005*, Kalayaan, London, p. 3.

135. Roberts at Twenty-first Century Slavery.

136. Courtesy of Kalayaan.

137. Courtesy of Kalayaan.

138. Break the Chain, www.ips-dc.org/campaign/stories.htm.

139. *Paladin Child*, Metropolitan Police, London, 2004, p. 1.

140. The following information is taken from an interview with Million Joseph conducted for this book in September 2006.

141. Kevin Bales, *Disposable People: New Slavery in the Global Economy*, University of California Press, Berkeley, 2004.

142. *Metro*, London, 11 July 2006.

143. Presentation by Guri Tyldum at the conference Twenty-first Century Slavery: Issues and Responses, Wilberforce Institute for the Study of Slavery and Emancipation, Hull, 23–24 November 2006.

144. Higher Education and Research Opportunities in the UK, www.hero. ac.uk/uk/inside_he/archives/2006/street_talking.cfm.

145. Interview with author, 30 June 2006.

146. http://news.bbc.co.uk/1/hi/programmes/4293669.stm.

147. 'Laura Agustin, Working in the European Sex Industry: Migrant Possibilities', June 2000, www.nswp.org/pdf/agustin-working.pdf.

148. H. Ward et al., 'Declining Prevalence of STI in the London Sex Indus-

try', in *Sexually Transmitted Infections*, British Medical Journals, London, March 2004, p. 375.

149. Annette Brunovskis and Guri Tyldum, *Crossing Borders: An Empirical Study of Transnational Prostitution and Trafficking in Human Beings*, Fafo, Oslo, 2004, pp. 30–32.

150. *Stopping Forced Labour*, ILO, Geneva, 2001, p. 50.

151. UNODC, *Trafficking in Persons: Global Patterns,* April 2006, p. 46.

152. *Trafficking in Persons Report*, US Department of State, Washington DC, June 2004, p6.

153. Ibid., p. 15.

154. UNODC, *Trafficking in Persons*, pp. 90–93.

155. *El País*, Madrid, 26 April 2006.

156. Gargi Bhattacharyya, *Traffick: The Illicit Movement of People and Things*, Pluto Press, London, 2005, pp. 176–8.

157. 1 August 2006.

158. www.spiegel.de/international/0,1518,404955,00.html.

159. Brunovskis and Tyldum, *Crossing Borders*, p. 65.

160. http://amnesty.org.uk/news_details.asp?NewsID=16890.

161. Author's interview with two ECP campaigners, 14 September 2006.

162. Ward et al., 'Declining Prevalence of STI in the London Sex Industry', p. 377.

163. Penelope Saunders, *Migration, Sex, Work and Trafficking in Persons*, www. walnet.org/csis/papers/saunders-migration.html.

Chapter 3

1. Jean-Pierre Garson, 'Ou travaillent les clandestins?', *L'OCDE Observateur*, Paris, December 1999.

2. Commission of the European Communities, *Report on the Functioning of the Transitional Arrangements Set Out in the 2003 Accession Treaty (period 1 May 2004–30 April 2006)*, Brussels, 2006, p. 11.

3 ITEM Club Special Report, *Finding Our Potential*, Ernst & Young, London, September 2006.

4. Although the term 'immigration' is used here, the authors are looking at recent years and so at those considered to be 'migrants' rather than immigrants for the purposes of this book.

5. Rebecca Riley and Martin Weale, 'Commentary: Immigration and its Effects', *National Institute Economic Review*, London, October 2006, p.9.

6. Home Office, *Accession Monitoring Report: May 2004–June 2006*, HMSO, London, 22 August 2006, p. 2.

7. IPPR press release, announcing publication of *Irregular Migration in the UK*, London, 31 March 2006.

8. See, for example, Dhananjayan Sriskandarajah, Laurence Cooley and Howard Reed, *Paying their Way: The Fiscal Contribution of Immigrants in the UK*, IPPR, London, April 2005; and Ceri Gott and Karl Johnston, *The Migrant Population in the UK: Fiscal Effects*, Home Office, London, 2002.

9. Cited in A. Green, D. Owen and R. Wilson, *Changing Patterns of Employment by Ethnic Group and for Migrant Workers*, Learning and Skills Council, London, November 2005, p. 8.

10. Precision Prospecting, *Temporary Workers in UK Agriculture and Horticulture: A Study of Employment Practices in the Agriculture and Horticulture Industry and Co-located Packhouse and Primary Food Processing Sectors*, Suffolk, 2004, p. 44.

11. Patrick Herman, 'Trafics de main d'œuvre couverts par l'État', *Le Monde Diplomatique*, Paris, June 2005.

12. Riley and Weale, 'Commentary: Immigration and its Effects', p. 9.

13. Ibid.

14. ITEM Club Special Report, *Finding Our Potential*, p. 12.

15. Commission of the European Communities, *Report on the Functioning of the Transitional Arrangements*, p. 13.

16. Ibid., p. 12.

17. See citations in J. Kempton et al., *Migrants in the UK: Their Characteristics and Labour Market Outcomes and Impacts*, Home Office, London, December 2002, p. 7.

18. CIPD, *Labour Market Outlook: Survey Report Autumn 2005*, London, 2005, p. 6.

19. Green et al., *Changing Patterns of Employment by Ethnic Group and for Migrant Workers*, p. 8.

20. Discussion with supermarket warehouse manager.

21. Dee Coombes, North Liverpool CAB, in conversation with author November 2006.

22. *OECD Observer*, Paris, February 2000.

23. Voice of America, 19 July 2006, www.voanews.com/english/archive/2006–07/IllegalImmigration2006–07–19–voa56.cfm?cfid=665 10737&cftoken=71243804.

24. Rakesh Kochhar, *Latino Labor Report, 2004*, Pew Hispanic Center, Washington DC, 2 May 2005, p. 2.

25. *Irish Examiner*, Cork, 20 November 2006.

26. *Daily Telegraph*, London, 30 October 2006.

27. *Financial Times*, London, 8 November 2006.

28. *Edinburgh Evening News*, Edinburgh, 6 September 2006.

29. *Rugby Advertiser*, Rugby, 28 September 2006.

30. *Newsnight*, BBC 2 television, 6 July 2006.

31. Homeless Link, *A8 National in London Homelessness Services*, London,

2006, p. 3.

32. *Peterborough Evening Telegraph*, Peterborough, 16 November 2006.

33. See, for example, *Daily Post*, Liverpool, 16 November 2006.

34. *Edinburgh Evening News*, 8 September 2006.

35. http://archive.thisischeshire.co.uk/2006/8/31/276443.html.

36. http://news.bbc.co.uk/1/hi/uk_politics/5119892.stm.

37. *Newsnight*, 6 July 2006.

38. *Lincolnshire Echo*, Lincoln, 15 June 2004.

39. Bridget Anderson et al., *Fair Enough? Central and East European Migrants in Low-wage Employment in the UK*, Joseph Rowntree Foundation, London, September 2006, p. 57.

40. http://web.worldbank.org/wbsite/external/news/0,,contentMDK: 2064 8762~menuPK:34480~page PK:64257043~piPK:437376~theSitePK:4607, 00.html.

41. Allasino et al., *Labour Market Discrimination against Migrant Workers in Italy*, p. 12.

42. Charalambos Kasimis, *Migrants in the Rural Economies of Greece and Southern Europe*', 1 October 2005, www.migrationinformation.org/feature/ print.cfm?ID=337.

43. Claudia Schneider et al., *A Profile of Migrant Workers in the Breckland Area*', Anglia Polytechnic University, July 2005, p. 3.

44. Unison, *International Labour Migration: A Unison Discussion Paper*, London, 2006, p. 9.

45. Ibid.

46. Ibid.

47. Ibid., p. 10.

48. Lualhati Roque, 'On the Losing End: The Migration of Filipino Health Professionals and the Decline of Health Care in the Philippines', paper presented at the 10th International Metropolis Conference, Toronto, 17–19 October 2005, p. 5.

49. *Newsnight*, 6 July 2006.

50. *Observer*, London, 15 May 2006.

51. *Le Monde Diplomatique*, Paris, December 2006.

52. Ibid.

Chapter 4

1. Ministerial statement to the House of Commons, 24 October 2006, http://www.ind.homeoffice.gov.uk/6353/21395/ministerialstatement 241006.pdf.

2. Home Office, *A Points-based System: Making Migration Work for Britain*, London, March 2006, www.homeoffice.gov.uk/documents/command-

points-based-migration?view=Binary, p. 15.

3. Ibid.

4. Ibid., p. 1.

5. Ibid., p. 29.

6. Ibid., p. 30.

7. JCWI, *Response of the JCWI to the Home Office Consultative Document 'Selective Admission: Making Migration Work for Britain'*, London, November 2005, p. 2.

8. Kalayaan, *Legalising Trafficking: The Cost of Making Migration Work for Britain*, London, March 2006, p. 1.

9. Commission of the European Communities, *Report on the Functioning of the Transitional Arrangements*.

10. http://news.bbc.co.uk/1/hi/england/london/6194410.stm.

11. *Irregular Migration in the UK*, IPPR, London, 2006., p. 13.

12. www.ind.homeoffice.gov.uk/aboutus/newsarchive/removalsatrecord high1.

13. http://press.homeoffice.gov.uk/press-releases/intelligence-led-units.

14. Humberside press release, 6 July 2006.

15. Interviews with author.

16. Home Office press release, 20 November 2006, www.ind.homeoffice. gov.uk/aboutus/newsarchive/smarterintelligentenforcement.

17. *Financial Times*, London, 22 January 2007.

18. See House of Lords debate, 1 November 2006, www.theyworkforyou. com/lords/?id=2006-11-01a.246.3.

19. Bridget Anderson et al., *Fair Enough? Central and East European Migrants in Low-wage Employment in the UK*, Joseph Rowntree Foundation, London, September 2006, pp. 110–11.

20. Remarks by Mark Boleat in a telephone interview for this book on 9 June 2006 and in his paper of May 2006, 'The Gangmasters (Licensing) Act 2004: Evaluation and Way Forward'.

21. Ibid.

22. Ibid.

23. Ibid., pp. 3–4.

24. *Guardian*, London, 7 August 2006.

Conclusion

1. *Guardian,* London, 10 February 2007.

2. Trades Union Congress, *The Hidden One-in-Five,* London, 2006, p. 1.

3. Robert Rowthorn, *The Economic Impact of Immigration*, Civitas Online Report, 2004, p. 1, www.civitas.org.uk/pdf/Rowthorn_Immigration.pdf.

Index